30 MINUTE
Rookie Cook

National Bestseller

Jean Paré

ORIGINAL SERIES

30-Minute
Rookie Cook

Jean Paré

www.companyscoming.com
visit our ✦ website

We gratefully acknowledge the following suppliers for their generous support of our Test and Photography Kitchens:

Broil King Barbecues
Corelle®
Hamilton Beach® Canada
Lagostina®
Proctor Silex® Canada
Tupperware®

Want cooking secrets?

Six *"sneak preview"* recipes are featured online **with every new book released.**

Visit us at ⬎
www.companyscoming.com

Table of Contents

Appetizers

Breakfasts &
Lunches

Salads & Soups

Sides

Go-Withs

Beef

Chicken

Fish & Seafood

Meatless

Pork & Lamb

Sweets & Treats

Foreword

In a world filled with fast-food restaurants and frozen dinners, it's easy to think a modern person can make it through life without ever really spending time in a kitchen.

We all know that today's world requires us to be on the run most of the time. A lot of on-the-go people like to say "I don't have time to cook," but the recipes in this book are designed to have you in the kitchen for only a short time. There's nothing wrong with  eating on the go once in a while, but preparing (and then later enjoying) a great meal shouldn't be seen as a chore. It's something you can have fun with. Turn on your favourite music and think of the kitchen not as a place of work, but as a creative space. You'll find that you can create a wholesome meal in the time it takes to watch an episode of your favourite show.

Learning to cook is something you can do as you go—and it's certainly a lot more fun than doing your taxes! With some simple guidance, *30-Minute Rookie Cook* will help you make great meals without a great deal of trouble. Think of the pride you'll feel eating and sharing meals with your guests knowing that you've prepared them yourself. And, boy, are these recipes guest-worthy! From impressive main dishes like Cheesy Portobellos, page 92, to sides like Cranberry Couscous, page 69, to desserts like Tiramisu Parfait, page 147, what guest wouldn't be pleased to accept your dinner invitation?

The recipes in this book were selected because they aren't complicated—they are designed to get novice cooks in the kitchen and creating meals in short order. No one expects you to put your life on hold as you learn how to cook. Instead, learn how easily cooking meals can fit into your busy schedule.

Jean Paré

Nutrition Information Guidelines

Each recipe is analyzed using the most current version of the Canadian Nutrient File from Health Canada, which is based on the United States Department of Agriculture (USDA) Nutrient Database.

- If more than one ingredient is listed (such as "butter or hard margarine"), or if a range is given (1 – 2 tsp., 5 – 10 mL), only the first ingredient or first amount is analyzed.

- For meat, poultry and fish, the serving size per person is based on the recommended 4 oz. (113 g) uncooked weight (without bone), which is 2 – 3 oz. (57 – 85 g) cooked weight (without bone)—approximately the size of a deck of playing cards.

- Milk used is 1% M.F. (milk fat), unless otherwise stated.

- Cooking oil used is canola oil, unless otherwise stated.

- Ingredients indicating "sprinkle," "optional," or "for garnish" are not included in the nutrition information.

- The fat in recipes and combination foods can vary greatly depending on the sources and types of fats used in each specific ingredient. For these reasons, the amount of saturated, monounsaturated and polyunsaturated fats may not add up to the total fat content.

Vera C. Mazurak, Ph.D.
Nutritionist

7

Your Guide to Good Cooking

Before you begin

Using recipes may seem pretty straightforward but there are a few tricks that make cooking so much easier:

1. **Read the recipe.** You wouldn't believe how many people don't do this. Our recipes are organized in a very logical manner. The ingredients are listed in the order you need them, and the cooking method is listed in a step-by-step manner—this means you don't have to worry about jumping back and forth in the recipe to figure out what you should be doing when.

2. **Make sure you understand all the cooking terms used.** Before turning on a burner or preheating an oven, know what you have to do. If you're not sure what "simmer" means, look it up first in the handy glossary we've included. Using the wrong cooking method may result in a truly regrettable meal.

3. **Collect all the utensils you'll need before you start.** There's nothing worse than having something simmering on the stove and realizing you can't add that all-important ingredient because you can't remember where you've left the measuring cup, or perhaps you can't even remember if you own a measuring cup!

4. **Collect and prepare all your ingredients before starting.** Nothing's more annoying than being halfway through making a meal, shaking out a bag of flour, and finding you have a quarter cup less than you need. Avoid those emergency trips to the grocery store by thinking of a recipe as a checklist first, and a guide second.

Tricky things about recipes

Every single recipe in this book has been prepared, tested and evaluated in our Company's Coming test kitchen, so we know they work and we love the way they taste. That being said, sometimes things go wrong when people use different types of equipment or ingredients, so keep in mind the following:

All microwaves aren't created equal...and the same goes for ovens. In the test kitchen, all our microwaves are 900 watts—but microwaves are sold in many different powers. You should be able to find the wattage of yours by opening the door and looking for the mandatory label. If your microwave is more than 900 watts, you may need to reduce the cooking time. If it's less than 900 watts, you'll probably need to increase the cooking time. The same goes for ovens—don't assume you can just put your food in for the maximum amount of time and everything will be fine.

It's over when it's over...except when it isn't. Many recipes will give time ranges for doneness ("bake for 25 to 35 minutes"). Make sure to check for doneness at the low end of the range (after 25 minutes). This will ensure that you are accounting for differences in ovens and microwaves and your food won't end up burned. In our recipes, we often give you hints as to when a product is done ("bake for 18 to 20 minutes until wooden pick inserted in centre of muffin comes out clean"). These clues will help you judge when your food is properly cooked. And if cooking meat makes you nervous, we highly recommend you invest in a meat thermometer that lists safe temperatures for cooking a variety of meats—it is the best way to make sure your meat will be safe to eat.

Accept no substitutions...most of the time. There are times when you may not have the exact ingredient and are wondering if the recipe will still work if you make a small substitution. In our books we often give you variations or suggestions for using different ingredients—whenever we do this, you'll be fine. In other cases, you're going to need to use common sense. For example, often it's OK to substitute frozen veggies for fresh—as long as they're thawed when you're ready to cook. But beware of replacing some ingredients with their "low-fat" or "light" varieties. Many low-fat products have higher water contents, which can mess with the final result—especially when it comes to baking.

Food safety essentials

With great cooking comes great responsibility. You don't want to be the person who gave all your dinner guests the extra gift of food poisoning at last week's get-together, so take care and heed the following points of advice:

- **Juices from raw meat or poultry are dangerous**—they need to be cleaned up right away. Always clean with soap and water after you've used a counter. Don't let food stains set, because they get a lot harder to clean when they harden. If you do the little cleaning jobs as you go, you will save yourself from having to spend hours cleaning a kitchen that has been neglected.
- **Don't keep using the same sponges or dishcloths**—they can collect bacteria and actually spread it around, rather than clean it up. Use paper towels if you can. If you prefer to use sponges, change them often. It doesn't take long for a sponge to soak up a laboratory's worth of bacteria. If you want to use cloth towels, remember to wash them often in hot water. If your home washer has a "sanitary" setting, that's what you should use for kitchen towels.
- **Good cooks always keep themselves clean.** Have some antibacterial hand soap ready by the sink, and wash your hands regularly as you cook. This may sound basic, but it's amazing how many people will handle raw meat or poultry and then toss salad greens without washing their hands. The same goes for the cutting board. Don't cut vegetables on it right after you've been chopping chicken. Cross-contamination equals food poisoning. And make sure to wash your utensils and cooking implements between different ingredients!
- **Don't thaw meat on the counter.** Sure, it might seem a lot faster to defrost a frozen steak at room temperature, but the safe method is to do it in the refrigerator. And keep a dish under your meat to catch falling juices.

- **Refrigerate and/or freeze leftover items right away.** Don't add sour cream to a recipe and leave the remainder out on the counter for hours. Make sure it goes back in the refrigerator right away. Think of it this way: every second food is not refrigerated, it is spoiling—so get it back into the fridge right away. The same goes with freezing. If you plan to freeze uneaten portions of the dish you just made, do it as soon as possible. Leaving food out not only causes it to spoil but it can also attract vermin— and nobody wants to be the person with a pest problem in the kitchen.

Time-saving strategies for easy cooking

The recipes in this book were designed to be easy to finish and not keep you in the kitchen for a long time. But we understand that we all have those days where it's hard to spare even half an hour to make a meal. On those days that you do have a little bit of extra time, you can do the following prep work to ensure you won't be wasting time when you are in a rush:

- Once a week, make sure to sit down and **plan meals** for the next seven days. From that list, make a list of grocery items you will need, and then do all the shopping in one fell swoop. This will save you from having to run to the grocery store every day.

- **Keep a running list of essentials** (such as sugar, flour and salt) on your refrigerator door. As soon as one of these items runs low, make a note of it so you will know to add it to your shopping list for the week. Keeping the kitchen well-stocked is the key to saving time.

- If you know you'll be hitting a spot where you will be pressed for time, working longer hours or have lots of family commitments, **make extra when you are cooking.** That way you can freeze the remainder and heat it up later. You can also take those extra meal portions to work with you. Not only will you get some comfort food at work, you'll save your money, too.

Items for a practical pantry

Below, we've listed the most common non-perishable or long-lasting items we've used in this book. They're great staples to have around the house for last-minute cooking. Often these items go on sale, so you can purchase them when the prices suit your pocketbook. And as far as the spices go, we suggest you buy small amounts of bulk spices and put them in small, labelled airtight containers. Buying spices this way costs a fraction of what buying bottles of spices costs.

Canned items
- beans • fruit • soup • vegetables

Dry items
- baking powder • baking soda • bread crumbs • cornstarch
- graham cracker crumbs • long grain rice • pasta and noodles

Oils, etc.
- cooking oil (we use canola oil) • olive oil • cooking spray

Spices, herbs & seasonings
- Cajun seasoning • cayenne pepper • chili powder • curry powder
- dried basil • dried crushed chilies • dried dillweed • dried oregano
- dried rosemary • dried thyme • dry mustard • garlic powder
- ground allspice • ground cinnamon • ground cloves • ground ginger
- ground nutmeg • Italian seasoning • lemon pepper
- Montreal steak spice • onion powder • paprika • parsley flakes
- poultry seasoning • seasoned salt • sesame seeds • taco seasoning

Miscellaneous
- barbecue sauce • basil pesto • chili paste (sambal oelek) • chili sauce
- cocoa powder • fancy mild molasses • hoisin sauce • honey
- hot pepper sauce • jams • ketchup • mango chutney • mayonnaise
- mustard • nuts • peanut butter • pizza, pasta & tomato sauces
- prepared beef broth • prepared chicken broth • salad dressings
- salsa • soy sauce • sun-dried tomato pesto • sweet chili sauce
- thick teriyaki basting sauce • tomato paste • vanilla extract • white vinegar • Worcestershire sauce

Essential kitchen equipment

Baking dish (glass) pan (metal)

Baking sheet

Blender or food processor

Bowls (mixing)

Bread knife

Broiler pan

Brush

Can opener

Casserole

Colander

Cookie sheet

Cutting board

Dry measures

Dutch oven

Electric mixer

Frying pan

Grater

Liquid measures

Measuring spoons

Meat thermometer

Mixing spoon

Muffin pan and mini-muffin pan

Pancake lifter

Pie plate

Pizza pan

Potato masher

Rubber spatula

Saucepan

Sharp knife

Sieve

Square baking pan

Vegetable peeler

Whisk

Wire rack

Wok

Cooking glossary

Below, we've compiled a list of cooking terms you may not be familiar with. The good thing with cooking is that the basic techniques are used over and over again—so the more you cook, the more your cooking knowledge will increase.

Batter: A thick or thin uncooked, pourable mixture.

Beat: Mixing or stirring ingredients together as rapidly as possible. You can do this manually or with an electric mixer.

Blot: Using a paper towel to absorb liquid from ingredients or to remove fat from fried food.

Broil: This is cooking using direct, high heat in an oven. The heat always comes from an overhead source. Every oven has a "broil" setting. You may be asked to move your oven rack closer to the top element so the food is nearer to the heat source. It is customary to leave your oven open a crack when broiling to prevent the food from baking.

Brown: This is the process of cooking an item in a greased pan so it quickly forms a brown crust which locks in flavour and juices. After a meat is browned, it will then be thoroughly cooked using a different cooking method.

Chop: A method of cutting food where the ingredient is cut into several pieces. The pieces do not necessarily have to be uniform, but they shouldn't vary greatly in size.

Cut in: When adding butter (or another solid fat) to a dry mixture, use a pastry blender or two knives to mix the butter only to the point where it is evenly spread through the ingredients. The butter or fat should be broken into small crumb-like pieces, with each piece totally covered in the dry ingredients.

Dice: This is the process of cutting food into small, equally-sized cube-shaped pieces. Dicing ensures even cooking of each morsel.

Doneness: When any food item is cooked well enough so it is safe to eat, it is "done." With meat, "doneness" can also indicate at what stage the diner prefers to eat the meat—rare, medium, well done, etc.

Drain: The removal of liquid or fat from food. The easiest way to drain food is to use a colander or mesh sieve.

Drippings: These are the juices that gather in the pan during the cooking of meat. The drippings can be used to make gravy or to fry other foods.

Drizzle: This is the process of pouring a very small amount of sauce, liquid or melted butter over food.

Fork-beaten: Using a fork to rapidly break up an ingredient.

Garnish: A garnish is an edible item, such as a fruit or an herb, that is added to a finished dish as a decoration.

14

Grate: A method of cutting by sliding a piece of solid food, usually cheese or a vegetable, against a grater. Graters may be sold with different holes and slots which produce different sizes of gratings from coarse to fine.

Grease: Applying a fat (such as cooking spray or butter) in a thin layer on a cooking surface before it is heated to prevent the food from sticking to the pan.

Halftime: The halfway point of the cooking process. In a lot of recipes, you will be asked to turn, check or add something to the food at halftime.

Jelly-roll style: You may be asked to roll flatter items in this manner. It simply means starting from one end and rolling while keeping the edges even.

Knead: The process of working dough into a smooth, putty-like mass by pressing down and folding in using the heels of your hands.

Let stand: If a recipe tells you to let something stand after cooking, simply place the food on a wire rack and leave it for the allotted time. Baked goods often need to stand so they don't lose their shape.

Mince: This is the process of cutting or grinding food into tiny pieces—usually much smaller than an 1/8 inch (3 mm) each.

Pinch: An amount of a dry ingredient that is too small to measure. A "pinch" is literally just that—use just what will fit in between your finger and thumb, and sprinkle it on the mixture.

Preheat: The turning on of an oven before food is placed in it. This is done so the oven can reach the cooking temperature specified in the recipe by the time the pan is ready to go in.

Process: Mixing or cutting up food using a blender or food processor.

Scramble-fry: To cook an item in a frying pan on medium or medium-high heat by continuously breaking it apart and redistributing it throughout the pan with a fork or a spatula.

Sift: This is the process of shaking dry ingredients through a fine mesh sieve to remove any lumps.

Simmer: After an item starts to boil, the heat is turned down to a medium-low temperature where it can gently bubble and continue to cook.

Slice: To cut food items, like apples or bread, into thinner portions.

Soften: Harder ingredients, like butter, may need to be softened so they're easier to work with. Soften by placing the ingredient on the counter, at room temperature, for about half an hour or microwaving for approximately 10 seconds.

Split: To cut items, usually buns or bread, straight down the middle, separating them into two halves.

Stir-fry: To cook food quickly in a hot frying pan or wok while stirring continuously.

Whisk: To mix ingredients using a whisk—a special wire instrument. Whisking is also a great way to break up lumps in dry ingredients.

15

Tropical Shrimp Dip

Send your taste buds to the tropics with this elegant dip that's perfect for your poshest company. Serve with rice crackers.

Butter (or hard margarine)	1 tbsp.	15 mL
Garlic clove, minced	1	1
(or 1/4 tsp., 1 mL, powder)		
Bag of frozen, uncooked shrimp (peeled and deveined), thawed and chopped	3/4 lb.	340 g
Can of pineapple tidbits, drained	14 oz.	398 mL
Barbecue sauce	1/3 cup	75 mL
Half-and-half cream	1/4 cup	60 mL
Medium unsweetened coconut	3 tbsp.	50 mL
Cayenne pepper	1/8 tsp.	0.5 mL
Chopped fresh parsley	1 tbsp.	15 mL

Melt butter in large frying pan on medium. Add garlic. Heat and stir for about 30 seconds until fragrant. Add shrimp. Heat and stir for about 1 minute until shrimp start to turn pink.

Add next 5 ingredients. Heat and stir for 1 to 2 minutes until hot and shrimp are pink. Do not overcook. Transfer to blender or food processor (see Safety Tip). Process with on/off motion until coarsely chopped. Transfer to serving bowl.

Sprinkle with parsley. Makes about 3 cups (750 mL).

1/4 cup (60 mL): 80 Calories; 3.3 g Total Fat (0.6 g Mono, 0.3 g Poly, 2.1 g Sat); 46 mg Cholesterol; 7 g Carbohydrate; 1 g Fibre; 6 g Protein; 104 mg Sodium

Safety Tip: Follow blender manufacturer's instructions for processing hot liquids. If in doubt, we recommend using a hand blender.

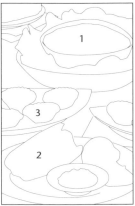

1. Speedy Sassy Salsa, page 79
2. Mega Meatball Sandwiches, page 88
3. Pecan Raisin Tarts, page 139

Props courtesy of: Pier 1 Imports
The Bay
Winners Stores

Shrimp Crostini

These crisp little toasts topped with a spicy, sweet and tangy shrimp mixture are highly addictive. If you're a fan of spice, be sure to double the amount of chili paste.

Baguette bread slices	48	48
(1/4 inch, 6 mm, thick)		
Cooking oil	1 tbsp.	15 mL
Frozen, cooked shrimp	1/4 lb.	113 g
(peeled and deveined),		
thawed and finely chopped		
Finely chopped yellow pepper	1/4 cup	60 mL
Seafood cocktail sauce	1/4 cup	60 mL
Finely chopped green onion	3 tbsp.	50 mL
Chili paste (sambal oelek)	1/2 tsp.	2 mL

Preheat oven to 400°F (205°C). Arrange baguette slices in single layer on ungreased baking sheet with sides. Lightly brush tops of baguette slices with cooking oil. Bake for about 10 minutes, turning at halftime, until golden and crisp.

Meanwhile, combine remaining 5 ingredients in small bowl. Spoon onto baguette slices. Makes 48 crostini.

1 crostini: 148 Calories; 0.8 g Total Fat (0.1 g Mono, 0.1 g Poly, trace Sat); 4 mg Cholesterol; 28 g Carbohydrate; 1 g Fibre; 5 g Protein; 361 mg Sodium

Pictured on page 18.

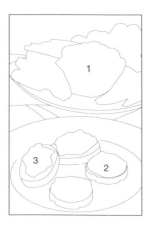

1. Brie Happy, page 21
2. Cucumber Hummus Rounds, page 20
3. Shrimp Crostini, above

Props courtesy of: Winners Stores

Green Olive Tapenade

Everyone will be green with envy when they see what a great cook you've become. Serve as a dip or as a spread for crackers or bread.

Large pitted green olives	1 cup	250 mL
Pine nuts, toasted (see Coach, page 63)	3 tbsp.	50 mL
Garlic cloves (or 1/2 tsp., 2 mL, powder)	2	2
Dried oregano	1 tsp.	5 mL
Ground cumin	1/4 tsp.	1 mL
Pepper	1/4 tsp.	1 mL
Olive (or cooking) oil	1/4 cup	60 mL
Turmeric	1/4 tsp.	1 mL

Put first 6 ingredients into blender or food processor. Process until finely chopped.

Add olive oil and turmeric. Process until just combined. Transfer to small bowl. Makes about 1 cup (250 mL).

2 tbsp. (30 mL): 123 Calories; 12.6 g Total Fat (8.7 g Mono, 2.4 g Poly, 1.2 g Sat); 0 mg Cholesterol; 3 g Carbohydrate; 1 g Fibre; 1 g Protein; 469 mg Sodium

Cucumber Hummus Rounds

Set your taste buds a-hummin' with this easy appetizer. Hummus is quite a different taste experience when paired with tangy yogurt and crisp, cool cucumber.

English cucumber slices (with peel), 1/4 inch (6 mm) thick	30	30
Salt, sprinkle		
Hummus	2/3 cup	150 mL
Plain yogurt	2/3 cup	150 mL
Sesame seeds, toasted (see Coach, page 63)	1 tbsp.	15 mL

Arrange cucumber slices on serving platter. Sprinkle with salt.

Spoon 1 tsp. (5 mL) hummus onto each cucumber slice. Spread evenly.

(continued on next page)

Appetizers

Spoon 1 tsp. (5 mL) yogurt over hummus on each slice. Sprinkle with sesame seeds. Makes 30 rounds.

1 round: 33 Calories; 1.2 g Total Fat (0.2 g Mono, 0.2 g Poly, 0.3 g Sat); 1 mg Cholesterol; 5 g Carbohydrate; 1 g Fibre; 2 g Protein; 25 mg Sodium

Pictured on page 18.

Brie Happy

What's not to Brie happy about? It's so easy to prepare this trendy dish. Serve with slices of apple, grapes or crackers. If you're really rushed, heat on medium power in the microwave for about two minutes.

Brie cheese round	4 oz.	125 g
Apricot jam	2 tbsp.	30 mL
Brown sugar, packed	1 1/2 tsp.	7 mL
Grated orange zest	1/4 tsp.	1 mL
Ground cinnamon	1/8 tsp.	0.5 mL
Sliced almonds, toasted (see Coach, page 63)	1 tbsp.	15 mL

Preheat oven to 325°F (160°C). Remove and discard rind from top of cheese. Place cheese round in small shallow baking dish.

Combine next 4 ingredients in small bowl. Spoon over cheese round. Bake for 10 to 12 minutes until cheese is softened and warm.

Sprinkle almonds over top. Serves 4.

1 serving: 127 Calories; 8.0 g Total Fat (2.7 g Mono, 0.5 g Poly, 4.4 g Sat); 25 mg Cholesterol; 9 g Carbohydrate; trace Fibre; 6 g Protein; 161 mg Sodium

Pictured on page 18.

Customize your Brie with your favourite flavours by trying other jams or jellies in place of the apricot jam. Apple or jalapeño jelly work great!

Beef-Stuffed Mushrooms

These two-bite mushrooms won't have your dinner guests too stuffed to indulge in your main course—but it may be hard to limit them to only a few!

Medium fresh whole white mushrooms	36	36
Cooking oil	1/2 tsp.	2 mL
Lean ground beef	1/4 lb.	113 g
Finely chopped onion	1/4 cup	60 mL
Ketchup	1 tbsp.	15 mL
Prepared horseradish	1 1/4 tsp.	6 mL
Celery salt	1/4 tsp.	1 mL
Garlic powder	1/4 tsp.	1 mL
Salt	1/4 tsp.	1 mL
Pepper	1/8 tsp.	0.5 mL
Grated Parmesan cheese	3 tbsp.	50 mL

Preheat broiler. Remove stems from mushrooms. Finely chop stems. Set aside. Arrange mushroom caps on ungreased baking sheet with sides. Broil on top rack in oven for about 3 minutes per side until browned. Set aside.

Preheat oven to 400°F (205°C). Heat cooking oil in large frying pan on medium-high. Add beef, onion and mushroom stems. Scramble-fry for about 5 minutes until beef is no longer pink. Drain.

Add next 6 ingredients. Stir. Spoon about 1/2 tsp. (2 mL) beef mixture into each mushroom cap.

Sprinkle with cheese. Bake for about 10 minutes until heated through. Makes 36 stuffed mushrooms.

1 stuffed mushroom: 24 Calories; 1.1 g Total Fat (0.4 g Mono, 0.1 g Poly, 0.6 g Sat); 4 mg Cholesterol; 1 g Carbohydrate; trace Fibre; 2 g Protein; 79 mg Sodium

Only wash your mushrooms prior to using. You can use a special mushroom brush to gently remove any dirt and then quickly rinse under water. Don't have a mushroom brush? A soft-bristled toothbrush works just as well.

Tuna Bruschetta

*Tuna adds a rather sophisticated dimension to bruschetta—
your guests will be pleasantly surprised.*

Olive (or cooking) oil	3 tbsp.	50 mL
Garlic cloves, minced	2	2
(or 1/2 tsp., 2 mL, powder)		
Baguette bread slices	48	48
(1/2 inch, 12 mm, thick)		
Can of chunk light tuna in water, drained	6 oz.	170 g
Finely chopped red onion	1/2 cup	125 mL
Large tomato, quartered, seeds removed,	1	1
finely chopped		
Finely chopped dill pickle	3 tbsp.	50 mL
Chopped fresh dill	2 tbsp.	30 mL
(or 1 1/2 tsp., 7 mL, dried)		
Lemon juice	2 tbsp.	30 mL
Creamed horseradish	1 tbsp.	15 mL
Olive (or cooking) oil	2 tsp.	10 mL
Salt	1/4 tsp.	1 mL
Pepper	1/4 tsp.	1 mL

Preheat broiler. Combine first amount of olive oil and garlic in small cup.
Brush on both sides of each baguette slice. Arrange in single layer on
ungreased baking sheet with sides. Broil on top rack in oven for about
1 minute per side until golden.

Combine remaining 10 ingredients in medium bowl. Spoon onto baguette
slices. Makes 48 bruschetta.

*1 bruschetta: 155 Calories; 1.6 g Total Fat (0.8 g Mono, 0.1 g Poly, 0.2 g Sat); 1 mg Cholesterol;
29 g Carbohydrate; 1 g Fibre; 6 g Protein; 357 mg Sodium*

COACH

If your oven is full of other appies and you can't
dedicate the toasting time, use pre-made crostini
instead of baguette slices.

Ham And Cheese Spirals

It won't be the swirly-twirly design that hypnotizes your guests,
it'll be the sublime savoury, yet sweet, taste.

Cream cheese, softened	4 oz.	125 g
Grated carrot	1/4 cup	60 mL
Ranch dressing	1/4 cup	60 mL
Flour tortillas (9 inch, 22 cm, diameter)	4	4
Deli ham slices (about 7 oz., 200 g)	4	4

Mash cream cheese with fork in small bowl. Add carrot and dressing. Stir well.

Spread cream cheese mixture evenly over each tortilla, almost to edge.

Place 1 ham slice over cream cheese mixture on each tortilla. Roll up tightly, jelly-roll style. Trim ends. Cut each roll diagonally into 8 slices. Makes 32 slices.

1 slice: 41 Calories; 2.7 g Total Fat (0.4 g Mono, 0.1 g Poly, 1.1 g Sat); 6 mg Cholesterol; 3 g Carbohydrate; trace Fibre; 1 g Protein; 106 mg Sodium

Bacon Mushroom Dip

If you're achin' for bacon, this is the dip for you. With bits of crisp bacon
and fried mushrooms, it goes great with raw vegetables or potato skins.

Bacon slices, diced	2	2
Finely chopped fresh white mushrooms	1 cup	250 mL
Sour cream	1 cup	250 mL
Mayonnaise	1/4 cup	60 mL
Finely chopped green onion	1 tbsp.	15 mL
Worcestershire sauce	1 tsp.	5 mL

Cook bacon in medium frying pan on medium for about 5 minutes until crisp. Transfer with slotted spoon to paper towel-lined plate to drain. Set aside.

(continued on next page)

Appetizers

Heat 1 tsp. (5 mL) drippings in same frying pan on medium. Add mushrooms. Cook for about 3 minutes, stirring occasionally, until liquid is evaporated. Spread mushrooms evenly on plate to cool.

Combine remaining 4 ingredients in medium bowl. Add bacon and mushrooms. Stir well. Makes about 1 1/2 cups (375 mL).

2 tbsp. (30 mL): 69 Calories; 6.3 g Total Fat (2.5 g Mono, 1.0 g Poly, 2.5 g Sat); 10 mg Cholesterol; 2 g Carbohydrate; trace Fibre; 1 g Protein; 66 mg Sodium

---

Chipotle Meatballs

Meatballs are surprisingly successful cocktail fare, and the smoky, sweet and spicy sauce they're coated in is sure to be a hit.

Box of frozen cooked meatballs	2 1/4 lbs.	1 kg
Salsa	2 cups	500 mL
Seedless raspberry jam	1 cup	250 mL
Coarsely chopped chipotle peppers in adobo sauce (see Coach, page 133)	2 tsp.	10 mL
Adobo sauce from chipotle peppers	1 tsp.	5 mL
Dried thyme	1/2 tsp.	2 mL
Chopped fresh parsley	1 tbsp.	15 mL

Put meatballs into Dutch oven. Heat on high for 2 minutes.

Meanwhile, put next 5 ingredients into blender or food processor. Process until smooth. Add to meatballs. Stir until coated. Bring to a boil. Reduce heat to medium. Boil gently, covered, for about 20 minutes, stirring often, until heated through. Transfer to serving bowl.

Sprinkle with parsley. Makes about 75 meatballs.

1 meatball: 41 Calories; 1.8 g Total Fat (0.8 g Mono, 0.1 g Poly, 0.6 g Sat); 11 mg Cholesterol; 4 g Carbohydrate; trace Fibre; 2 g Protein; 61 mg Sodium

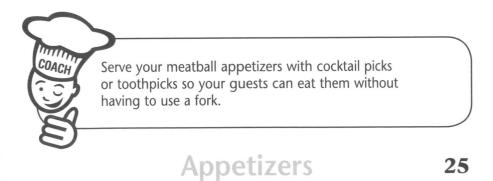

COACH

Serve your meatball appetizers with cocktail picks or toothpicks so your guests can eat them without having to use a fork.

Baja Bean Dip

This bean dip is unexpectedly refreshing. Smooth and creamy,
it goes especially well with crisp veggies or tortilla chips.

Can of white kidney beans, rinsed and drained	19 oz.	540 mL
Chopped fresh cilantro or parsley	1/4 cup	60 mL
Olive (or cooking) oil	3 tbsp.	50 mL
Lime juice	2 tbsp.	30 mL
Finely chopped fresh jalapeño pepper (see Coach, page 75)	1 tbsp.	15 mL
Ground cumin	1 tsp.	5 mL
Dried oregano	1/2 tsp.	2 mL
Salt	1/2 tsp.	2 mL
Pepper	1/2 tsp.	2 mL

Sprig of fresh cilantro or parsley, for garnish

Put first 9 ingredients into blender or food processor. Process, scraping down sides if necessary, until smooth. Transfer to serving bowl.

Garnish with cilantro sprig. Makes about 1 3/4 cups (425 mL).

1/4 cup (60 mL): 112 Calories; 6.4 g Total Fat (4.2 g Mono, 0.5 g Poly, 0.8 g Sat); 0 mg Cholesterol; 11 g Carbohydrate; 3 g Fibre; 4 g Protein; 189 mg Sodium

Red Hot Chicken Bites

Rather than going down to the pub to watch the next big game,
why not bake up a batch of these fiery snacks and invite the gang to your place?
Ranch dressing for dipping and a cold beer to wash them down are optional—
but definitely recommended!

Grated Parmesan cheese	6 tbsp.	100 mL
Fine dry bread crumbs	1/4 cup	60 mL
Cajun seasoning	1/2 tsp.	2 mL
Garlic powder	1/4 tsp.	1 mL
Boneless, skinless chicken thighs, cut into bite-sized pieces	3/4 lb.	340 g
Louisiana hot sauce	2 tbsp.	30 mL

(continued on next page)

Preheat oven to 375°F (190°C). Combine first 4 ingredients in medium bowl.

Put chicken into separate medium bowl. Drizzle hot sauce over top. Stir until coated. Add to crumb mixture in 3 batches. Toss until coated. Arrange in single layer on greased baking sheet with sides. Bake for about 20 minutes, turning at halftime, until golden and no longer pink inside. Makes about 30 delicious bites for the whole gang.

1 bite: 55 Calories; 3.1 g Total Fat (1.1 g Mono, 0.3 g Poly, 1.5 g Sat); 16 mg Cholesterol; 1 g Carbohydrate; trace Fibre; 6 g Protein; 165 mg Sodium

---

Fire-Spiced Hot Wings

Watch out, folks: we aren't kidding, these babies are hot! Arm yourself with a whole bunch of napkins and something to cool the fiery heat.

Louisiana hot sauce	1/3 cup	75 mL
Lime juice	1/4 cup	60 mL
Soy sauce	1/4 cup	60 mL
Pepper	1 tsp.	5 mL
Cayenne pepper	1/2 tsp.	2 mL
Garlic powder	1/2 tsp.	2 mL
Split chicken wings, tips discarded (or chicken drumettes)	2 lbs.	900 g

Preheat oven to 450°F (230°C). Combine first 6 ingredients in 1 cup (250 mL) liquid measure. Transfer 1/3 cup (75 mL) to small bowl. Set aside.

Put wing pieces into large resealable freezer bag. Add remaining hot sauce mixture. Seal bag. Toss until coated. Drain. Arrange wing pieces on greased wire rack set in foil-lined baking sheet with sides. Bake for about 15 minutes, turning at halftime, until tender and no longer pink inside. Remove from oven. Preheat broiler. Brush wing pieces with reserved hot sauce mixture. Broil on centre rack in oven for about 4 minutes until browned. Makes about 24 wing pieces (or 16 drumettes).

1 wing: 116 Calories; 8.2 g Total Fat (3.1 g Mono, 2.1 g Poly, 2.1 g Sat); 31 mg Cholesterol; trace Carbohydrate; trace Fibre; 10 g Protein; 33 mg Sodium

Orange Chipper Muffins

You'll be feeling rather chipper yourself after you try these muffins—the flavours of orange and chocolate pair perfectly. Your blender will make quick work of chopping the orange—and adding the peel gives extra health benefits.

All-purpose flour	2 cups	500 mL
Cocoa, sifted if lumpy	1 tbsp.	15 mL
Baking powder	1 1/2 tsp.	7 mL
Baking soda	1 tsp.	5 mL
Salt	1/4 tsp.	1 mL
Large unpeeled orange, cut into eight wedges, seeds removed	1	1
Large eggs	2	2
Granulated sugar	1 cup	250 mL
Butter (or hard margarine), softened	1/2 cup	125 mL
Mini semi-sweet chocolate chips	3/4 cup	175 mL

Preheat oven to 375°F (190°C). Measure first 5 ingredients into large bowl. Stir. Make a well in centre.

Put orange wedges into blender or food processor. Process with on/off motion until finely chopped. Add next 3 ingredients. Process until smooth. Add to well.

Add chocolate chips. Stir until just moistened. Fill 12 greased muffin cups 3/4 full. Bake for 18 to 20 minutes until wooden pick inserted in centre of muffin comes out clean. Let stand in pan for 5 minutes. Remove muffins from pan and place on wire rack to cool. Makes 12 muffins.

1 muffin: 287 Calories; 12.5 g Total Fat (3.7 g Mono, 0.6 g Poly, 7.6 g Sat); 51 mg Cholesterol; 42 g Carbohydrate; 2 g Fibre; 4 g Protein; 251 mg Sodium

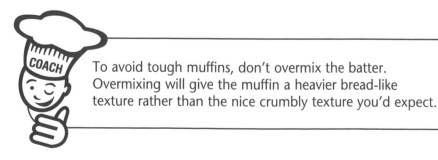

COACH To avoid tough muffins, don't overmix the batter. Overmixing will give the muffin a heavier bread-like texture rather than the nice crumbly texture you'd expect.

Protein Power Shake

Energy abounds with these peachy protein-packed shakes!

Can of sliced peaches in light syrup (with syrup)	14 oz.	398 mL
Milk	1 cup	250 mL
Package of peach dessert tofu	5 1/3 oz.	150 g
Liquid honey	1 tbsp.	15 mL
Vanilla extract (optional)	1/4 tsp.	1 mL

Put all 5 ingredients into blender. Process until smooth. Makes about 3 1/2 cups (875 mL).

1 cup (250 mL): 172 Calories; 1.6 g Total Fat (0.3 g Mono, 0.1 g Poly, 0.5 g Sat); 4 mg Cholesterol; 38 g Carbohydrate; 2 g Fibre; 5 g Protein; 48 mg Sodium

Pepperoni Pizza Bagels

Use your favourite pizza toppings to customize this bagel beauty.

Pizza sauce	2 tbsp.	30 mL
Plain bagel, split	1	1
Grated mozzarella cheese	1/3 cup	75 mL
Chopped pepperoni	3 tbsp.	50 mL

Preheat oven to 400°F (205°C). Spread pizza sauce evenly over cut sides of bagel. Place, cut-side up, on greased baking sheet with sides.

Sprinkle cheese over sauce. Sprinkle pepperoni over top. Bake for about 10 minutes until cheese is melted and bubbly. Makes 2 pizza bagels.

1 pizza bagel: 291 Calories; 14.6 g Total Fat (5.9 g Mono, 1.4 g Poly, 6.1 g Sat); 32 mg Cholesterol; 26 g Carbohydrate; 1 g Fibre; 13 g Protein; 811 mg Sodium

Freeze leftover pizza sauce in ice cube trays (about 2 tbsp., 30 mL, sauce in each) to use at another time.

Brunch Special

Although this special treat would be perfect served on Christmas morn, its decadent, creamy sauce and the combination of scrambled eggs, ham and asparagus will make any morning a special occasion.

Large eggs	8	8
Milk	1/4 cup	60 mL
Can of condensed cream of asparagus soup	10 oz.	284 mL
Milk	1/2 cup	125 mL
Butter (or hard margarine)	1 tbsp.	15 mL
Chopped fresh asparagus	1 cup	250 mL
Diced cooked ham	1 cup	250 mL
Plain English muffins, split	4	4
Grated medium Cheddar cheese	1/2 cup	125 mL

Beat eggs and first amount of milk in small bowl. Set aside.

Combine soup and second amount of milk in small saucepan. Heat on medium for about 5 minutes, stirring often, until hot but not boiling. Cover to keep warm.

Meanwhile, melt butter in large frying pan on medium. Add asparagus and ham. Heat and stir for about 3 minutes until asparagus is tender-crisp. Add egg mixture. Cook for about 4 minutes, stirring constantly with spatula and scraping sides and bottom of pan, until eggs are set and liquid is evaporated. Stir in soup mixture.

Toast English muffins halves. Spoon egg mixture over muffin halves.

Sprinkle with cheese. Serves 4.

1 serving: 539 Calories; 29.0 g Total Fat (9.2 g Mono, 2.3 g Poly, 11.5 g Sat); 432 mg Cholesterol; 36 g Carbohydrate; 3 g Fibre; 34 g Protein; 950 mg Sodium

Curried Waldorf Chicken Wraps

If you're too wrapped up to step out and grab lunch, make this super-quick wrap instead! This also works great as appetizer fare—simply stuff the filling into small pitas.

Mayonnaise	1/2 cup	125 mL
Lemon juice	2 tsp.	10 mL
Curry powder	1/2 tsp.	2 mL
Grated lemon zest	1/2 tsp.	2 mL
Salt	1/4 tsp.	1 mL
Pepper	1/4 tsp.	1 mL
Chopped cooked chicken (see Coach, below)	2 cups	500 mL
Chopped unpeeled apple	1 cup	250 mL
Chopped celery	3/4 cup	175 mL
Chopped walnuts	1/4 cup	60 mL
Lettuce leaves	6	6
Flour tortillas (9 inch, 22 cm, diameter)	6	6

Combine first 6 ingredients in medium bowl.

Add next 4 ingredients. Stir until coated.

Place 1 lettuce leaf on each tortilla. Spoon chicken mixture down centre of leaves. Fold bottom ends of tortillas over filling. Fold in sides, slightly overlapping, leaving top ends open. Place, seam-side down, on plate. Makes 6 wraps.

1 wrap: 389 Calories; 21.3 g Total Fat (7.4 g Mono, 6.6 g Poly, 3.2 g Sat); 49 mg Cholesterol; 32 g Carbohydrate; 2 g Fibre; 19 g Protein; 587 mg Sodium

Don't have any leftover chicken? Start with two boneless, skinless chicken breast halves (4 – 6 oz., 113 – 170 g, each). Place in a large frying pan with 1 cup (250 mL) water or chicken broth. Simmer, covered, for 12 to 14 minutes until no longer pink inside. Drain. Chop. Makes about 2 cups (500 mL) of cooked chicken.

Denver Noodle Frittata

A noodle frittata? It works! Noodles add texture
to this familiar-tasting, family-friendly frittata.

Water	4 cups	1 L
Salt	1/2 tsp.	2 mL
Tiny shell pasta	1 cup	250 mL
Cooking oil	1 tbsp.	15 mL
Diced cooked ham	3/4 cup	175 mL
Chopped green pepper	1/2 cup	125 mL
Chopped onion	1/2 cup	125 mL
Large eggs	6	6
Salt	1/4 tsp.	1 mL
Cayenne pepper	1/8 tsp.	0.5 mL
Grated medium Cheddar cheese	1 cup	250 mL
Chopped fresh parsley	1 tbsp.	15 mL

Combine water and salt in medium saucepan. Bring to a boil. Add pasta. Boil, uncovered, for 6 to 8 minutes, stirring occasionally, until tender but firm. Drain. Return to same pot. Cover to keep warm.

Meanwhile, heat cooking oil in medium frying pan on medium. Add next 3 ingredients. Cook for about 5 minutes, stirring occasionally, until onion is tender-crisp. Add pasta. Stir. Spread evenly in pan.

Preheat broiler. Beat next 3 ingredients with fork in medium bowl. Pour over pasta mixture. Reduce heat to medium-low. Cook, covered, for about 5 minutes until bottom is golden and top is almost set. Remove from heat.

Sprinkle cheese over top. Broil on centre rack in oven (see Coach, page 95) for 2 to 4 minutes until cheese is melted and golden.

Sprinkle with parsley. Cuts into 4 wedges.

1 wedge: 544 Calories; 25.5 g Total Fat (9.9 g Mono, 2.8 g Poly, 10.4 g Sat); 332 mg Cholesterol; 47 g Carbohydrate; 2 g Fibre; 31 g Protein; 432 mg Sodium

Pictured on page 35.

Turkey Pita

Get fresh pitas from the local Lebanese or Greek bakery
to use in this tasty wrap. A great lunch to take to work or school—
just remember to keep it cool until you're ready to eat.

Salad dressing (or mayonnaise)	1 tbsp.	15 mL
Sun-dried tomato pesto	1 tsp.	5 mL
Pita bread (7 inch, 18 cm, diameter)	1	1
Lettuce leaves	4	4
Grated medium Cheddar cheese	1/4 cup	60 mL
Tomato slices	4	4
Deli turkey breast slices	3 oz.	85 g

Combine dressing and pesto in small cup. Spread evenly over pita.

Arrange lettuce leaves over pesto mixture. Sprinkle with cheese. Arrange tomato slices in a row from top to bottom. Place turkey slices over tomato. Fold in sides, leaving ends open. Place, seam-side down, on plate. Makes 1 pita.

1 pita: 443 Calories; 18.0 g Total Fat (6.9 g Mono, 3.2 g Poly, 6.8 g Sat); 60 mg Cholesterol; 44 g Carbohydrate; 3 g Fibre; 27 g Protein; 1587 mg Sodium

Pictured on page 35.

TURKEY WRAP: Use a flour tortilla instead of pita bread.

Meatza Pizza

This manly meat masterpiece is sure to put any pizzeria to shame.
Ordinary pizza sauce not macho enough for you? We've used
barbecue sauce, a natural fit with all your favourite meats.

Prebaked pizza crust	1	1
(12 inch, 30 cm, diameter)		
Barbecue sauce	1/3 cup	75 mL
Chopped cooked ham	1 cup	250 mL
Chopped cooked roast beef (see Note)	1 cup	250 mL
Chopped pepperoni	1 cup	250 mL
Grated mozzarella cheese	1 3/4 cups	425 mL

Preheat oven to 425°F (220°C). Place crust on greased 12 inch (30 cm) pizza pan. Spread barbecue sauce evenly over crust.

Sprinkle next 3 ingredients over sauce.

Sprinkle cheese over top. Bake for about 10 minutes until heated through and cheese is golden. Cuts into 8 wedges.

1 wedge: 254 Calories; 16.3 g Total Fat (6.5 g Mono, 1.2 g Poly, 7.2 g Sat); 48 mg Cholesterol; 6 g Carbohydrate; 1 g Fibre; 19 g Protein; 537 mg Sodium

Pictured on page 35.

Note: If you don't have any leftover roast beef, use deli roast beef slices instead.

1. Meatza Pizza, above
2. Turkey Pita, page 33
3. Denver Noodle Frittata, page 32

Props courtesy of: The Bay

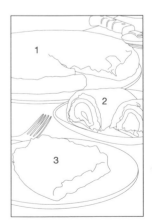

Peachy-Keen Crepe

If you're keen on crepes but a little afraid to make them, try these effort-free crepes that bake in your oven. Watch the crepe reach great heights as it bakes (it'll deflate when it's out of the oven). It's just peachy!

Large eggs	2	2
Milk	1/2 cup	125 mL
Butter (or hard margarine), melted	2 tbsp.	30 mL
All-purpose flour	1/2 cup	125 mL
Salt	1/4 tsp.	1 mL
Can of sliced peaches in syrup, drained	14 oz.	398 mL
Maple (or maple-flavoured) syrup	1/3 cup	75 mL

Preheat oven to 450°F (230°C). Place 9 x 9 inch (22 x 22 cm) pan in oven. Whisk first 3 ingredients in medium bowl.

Add flour and salt. Beat until smooth. Spray hot pan with cooking spray. Pour batter into pan. Bake for about 12 minutes until edges are browned and middle is puffed up.

Meanwhile, combine peaches and syrup in small bowl. Cut crepe into 4 equal portions. Spoon peach mixture over top. Serves 4.

1 serving: 295 Calories; 8.7 g Total Fat (2.7 g Mono, 0.6 g Poly, 4.6 g Sat); 110 mg Cholesterol; 50 g Carbohydrate; 2 g Fibre; 6 g Protein; 241 mg Sodium

Pictured on page 36.

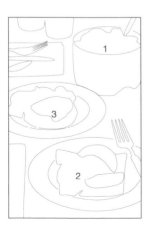

1. Fresh Breakfast Salad, page 38
2. Peachy-Keen Crepe, above
3. Easy Eggs Benny, page 41

Props courtesy of: Pier 1 Imports
Stokes

Fresh Breakfast Salad

After a long, restful sleep, refresh yourself with this fantastic salad. Great for brunches, lunches or snacks. Don't be afraid to change it up with your favourite fruits, as long as you use the same amounts as called for in the recipe.

Fresh strawberries, halved	2 1/2 cups	625 mL
Medium bananas, sliced	2	2
Medium peeled oranges, halved and sliced	2	2
Orange juice	1/4 cup	60 mL
Liquid honey	2 tbsp.	30 mL
Sliced almonds, toasted (see Coach, page 63), optional	2 tbsp.	30 mL

Put first 3 ingredients into medium bowl.

Combine orange juice and honey in small bowl. Drizzle over fruit mixture. Toss gently.

Sprinkle almonds over top. Makes about 4 cups (1 L).

1 cup (250 mL): 159 Calories; 0.6 g Total Fat (0.1 g Mono, 0.2 g Poly, 0.1 g Sat); 0 mg Cholesterol; 40 g Carbohydrate; 4 g Fibre; 2 g Protein; 2 mg Sodium

Pictured on page 36.

Tropical Burst

Give yourself a burst of morning energy with this sweet, refreshing smoothie. Perfect for those grab-and-go mornings.

Frozen overripe medium banana (see Coach, page 39), cut up	1	1
Apple juice	1 cup	250 mL
Vanilla frozen yogurt	1/4 cup	60 mL
Medium unsweetened coconut	1 tbsp.	15 mL

Put all 4 ingredients into blender. Process until smooth. Makes about 1 3/4 cups (425 mL).

1 cup (250 mL): 174 Calories; 3.2 g Total Fat (0.4 g Mono, 0.2 g Poly, 2.3 g Sat); trace Cholesterol; 37 g Carbohydrate; 2 g Fibre; 2 g Protein; 29 mg Sodium

Buttery Orange Scones

Sweet, rich scones are a wonderful addition to morning coffee or tea. The simple addition of orange zest adds a subtle, yet complex, new dimension. Give your co-workers some special attention and bring these in for a morning treat.

All-purpose flour	1 3/4 cups	425 mL
Granulated sugar	1/2 cup	125 mL
Baking powder	2 tsp.	10 mL
Salt	1/2 tsp.	2 mL
Cold butter (or hard margarine), cut up	1/3 cup	75 mL
Large egg, fork-beaten	1	1
Milk	1/3 cup	75 mL
Grated orange zest	1 tsp.	5 mL
Granulated sugar	2 tsp.	10 mL

Preheat oven to 375°F (190°C). Combine first 4 ingredients in large bowl. Cut in butter until mixture resembles coarse crumbs. Make a well in centre.

Combine next 3 ingredients in small bowl. Add to well. Stir until soft dough forms. Turn out onto lightly floured surface. Knead 6 times. Pat out to 6 inch (15 cm) square, about 3/4 inch (2 cm) thick.

Sprinkle second amount of sugar over top. Cut into nine 2 × 2 inch (5 × 5 cm) squares. Arrange squares 2 inches (5 cm) apart on greased baking sheet. Bake for 15 to 20 minutes until edges are golden. Makes 9 scones.

1 scone: 196 Calories; 7.4 g Total Fat (2.0 g Mono, 0.3 g Poly, 4.5 g Sat); 39 mg Cholesterol; 30 g Carbohydrate; trace Fibre; 3 g Protein; 247 mg Sodium

When your bananas get too ripe to enjoy fresh, peel and cut them into 2 inch (5 cm) chunks and freeze on a baking sheet. Once frozen, transfer to a freezer bag for use in any blended beverage. Ripe bananas have superior flavour for beverages.

Quick Quiche Squares

A bacon and red pepper quiche can come together at quantum speeds—when it's in biscuit form. Serve with salad for lunch, or toast for brunch.

Chopped onion	1/2 cup	125 mL
Bacon slices, diced	3	3
Large eggs	3	3
Biscuit mix	2/3 cup	150 mL
Milk	1/2 cup	125 mL
Salt	1/4 tsp.	1 mL
Grated Swiss cheese	1 cup	250 mL
Chopped roasted red pepper	1/2 cup	125 mL

Preheat oven to 400°F (205°C). Cook onion and bacon in large frying pan on medium-high for 2 to 4 minutes until bacon is browned.

Meanwhile, whisk next 4 ingredients in large bowl until smooth.

Add cheese, red pepper and bacon mixture. Stir. Pour into greased 9 × 9 inch (22 × 22 cm) baking dish. Bake for about 20 minutes until set and knife inserted in centre comes out clean. Cuts into 6 squares.

1 square: 295 Calories; 17.9 g Total Fat (6.7 g Mono, 1.7 g Poly, 8.4 g Sat); 119 mg Cholesterol; 20 g Carbohydrate; 1 g Fibre; 12 g Protein; 604 mg Sodium

COACH

Don't worry about roasting your own peppers—you can get jars of them in the same aisle you'd find pickles.

Easy Eggs Benny

*We've simplified hollandaise sauce so you can enjoy the great taste
of eggs Benedict whenever you like. This recipe can also
be made with fried eggs if you prefer not to poach them.*

Water, approximately	4 cups	1 L
White vinegar	2 tsp.	10 mL
Large eggs	4	4
Mayonnaise	2 tbsp.	30 mL
Plain yogurt	2 tbsp.	30 mL
Dijon mustard	1/2 tsp.	2 mL
Lemon juice	1/4 tsp.	1 mL
Paprika, just a pinch		
Plain English muffins, split	2	2
Deli ham slices (about 3 oz., 85 g)	4	4

Pour water into medium saucepan until about 1 1/2 inches (3.8 cm) deep.
Add vinegar. Stir. Bring to a boil. Reduce heat to medium. Water should
continue to simmer. Break 1 egg into shallow dish. Slip egg into water.
Repeat with remaining eggs. Cook for 2 to 3 minutes until egg whites
are set and yolks reach desired doneness. Remove eggs with slotted spoon.
Blot dry with paper towels.

Meanwhile, combine next 5 ingredients in small bowl.

Toast English muffin halves. Place 1 ham slice on each muffin half.
Place eggs over ham. Top with yogurt mixture. Serves 4.

*1 serving: 202 Calories; 9.7 g Total Fat (4.3 g Mono, 2.0 g Poly, 2.1 g Sat); 199 mg Cholesterol;
15 g Carbohydrate; 1 g Fibre; 13 g Protein; 509 mg Sodium*

Pictured on page 36.

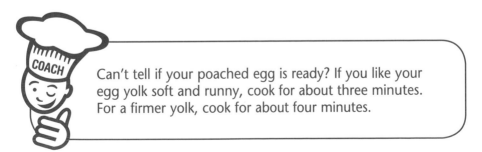

COACH

Can't tell if your poached egg is ready? If you like your
egg yolk soft and runny, cook for about three minutes.
For a firmer yolk, cook for about four minutes.

Blueberry Lemon Muffins

This classic morning treat is all jazzed up with a hint of lemon.
Use the juice from your lemon to make soured milk for this recipe.

All-purpose flour	2 cups	500 mL
Granulated sugar	3/4 cup	175 mL
Baking powder	2 tsp.	10 mL
Baking soda	1/2 tsp.	2 mL
Salt	1/2 tsp.	2 mL
Large egg, fork-beaten	1	1
Buttermilk (or soured milk, see Coach, below)	1 cup	250 mL
Butter (or hard margarine), melted	1/3 cup	75 mL
Grated lemon zest	1 tsp.	5 mL
Vanilla extract	1 tsp.	5 mL
Fresh (or frozen) blueberries	1 cup	250 mL

Preheat oven to 400°F (205°C). Measure first 5 ingredients into large bowl. Stir. Make a well in centre.

Combine next 5 ingredients in medium bowl. Add to well.

Add blueberries. Stir until just moistened. Fill 24 mini-muffin cups 3/4 full. Bake for 12 to 14 minutes until wooden pick inserted in centre of muffin comes out clean. Let stand in pan for 5 minutes. Remove muffins from pan and place on wire rack to cool. Makes 24 mini-muffins.

1 mini-muffin: 90 Calories; 2.8 g Total Fat (0.1 g Mono, trace Poly, 1.7 g Sat); 15 mg Cholesterol; 15 g Carbohydrate; trace Fibre; 2 g Protein; 130 mg Sodium

COACH To make soured milk, measure 1 tbsp. (15 mL) white vinegar or lemon juice into a 1 cup (250 mL) liquid measure. Add enough milk to make 1 cup (250 mL). Stir. Let stand for 1 minute.

Baked French Toast

Do you ever wish that you could do a whole bunch of things at one time? Well, this recipe helps you multi-task. You can bake your French toast while you read the morning paper—no one will know you weren't slaving over a hot stove!

Large eggs	8	8
Can of evaporated milk	13 1/2 oz.	385 mL
Granulated sugar	1 tbsp.	15 mL
Vanilla extract	1 tsp.	5 mL
Ground cinnamon	1/2 tsp.	2 mL
Butter (or hard margarine), melted	2 tbsp.	30 mL
Day-old French bread slices	12	12
(1 inch, 2.5 cm, thick)		
Can of apple pie filling	19 oz.	540 mL
Maple (or maple-flavoured) syrup	1/2 cup	125 mL
Ground cinnamon	1 tsp.	5 mL
Icing (confectioner's) sugar	2 tbsp.	30 mL

Preheat oven to 425°F (220°C). Whisk eggs in large bowl until frothy. Add next 4 ingredients. Whisk until well combined.

Brush 10 x 15 inch (25 x 38 cm) baking sheet with sides with butter. Dip 1 bread slice into egg mixture. Turn to coat both sides. Place on baking sheet. Repeat with remaining bread slices and egg mixture. Pour remaining egg mixture over top. Bake for about 15 minutes until golden.

Meanwhile, combine next 3 ingredients in medium saucepan. Heat and stir on medium until heated through. Cover to keep warm.

Transfer toast to large serving platter. Sprinkle icing sugar over top. Serve apple mixture on the side. Serves 4.

1 serving: 865 Calories; 21.0 g Total Fat (7.7 g Mono, 2.6 g Poly, 8.6 g Sat); 395 mg Cholesterol; 140 g Carbohydrate; 5 g Fibre; 29 g Protein; 986 mg Sodium

Steak Salads

A great example of how to turn a salad into a meal. If you aren't in a rush, you can easily wash and cut your own lettuce (it's a lot cheaper). And if you love horseradish, double the amount.

Cooking oil	1 tbsp.	15 mL
Beef top sirloin steak	3/4 lb.	340 g
Seasoned salt, sprinkle		
Iceberg lettuce mix, lightly packed	8 cups	2 L
Snow peas, trimmed and halved	1 cup	250 mL
Grated medium Cheddar cheese	1/2 cup	125 mL
Thinly sliced green onion	1/4 cup	60 mL
Coleslaw dressing	1/3 cup	75 mL
Prepared horseradish	1 tsp.	5 mL

Heat cooking oil in large frying pan on medium-high. Sprinkle both sides of steak with seasoned salt. Add to frying pan. Cook for about 3 minutes per side until desired doneness. Transfer to cutting board. Let stand for 10 minutes. Cut into short, thin strips.

Meanwhile, put next 4 ingredients into large bowl.

Combine dressing and horseradish in small cup. Drizzle over lettuce mixture. Toss. Arrange on 4 salad plates. Arrange steak over top. Makes 4 salads.

1 salad: 323 Calories; 20.4 g Total Fat (5.8 g Mono, 1.5 g Poly, 6.6 g Sat); 67 mg Cholesterol; 10 g Carbohydrate; 1 g Fibre; 24 g Protein; 294 mg Sodium

Salads & Soups

Artichoke Rotini Salad

The addition of artichokes to this pasta salad makes it trés *chic.*
The unique spirals of rotini pasta are great for gripping creamy sauces.

Water	6 cups	1.5 L
Salt	3/4 tsp.	4 mL
Rotini pasta	2 cups	500 mL
Jar of marinated artichoke hearts, drained and liquid reserved, chopped	6 oz.	170 mL
Chopped celery	1/2 cup	125 mL
Chopped green onion	1/3 cup	75 mL
Roasted red peppers, blotted dry and chopped	1/4 cup	60 mL
Mayonnaise	1/2 cup	125 mL
Reserved liquid from artichoke hearts	1/4 cup	60 mL

Combine water and salt in large saucepan or Dutch oven. Bring to a boil. Add pasta. Boil, uncovered, for about 10 minutes, stirring occasionally, until tender but firm. Drain. Rinse with cold water. Drain well. Transfer to large bowl.

Add next 4 ingredients. Toss.

Combine mayonnaise and reserved marinade in small bowl. Add to pasta mixture. Toss until coated. Makes about 3 1/2 cups (875 mL).

1 cup (250 mL): 675 Calories; 18.5 g Total Fat (9.1 g Mono, 5.5 g Poly, 1.7 g Sat); 9 mg Cholesterol; 108 g Carbohydrate; 6 g Fibre; 20 g Protein; 434 mg Sodium

Thai Chicken Salad

This salad's sure to be the "mein" attraction on your dinner table! Crunchy chow mein noodles crown chicken and fresh greens coated in a dressing of cilantro, peanut, ginger and soy. And for an extra neat treat, try the dressing on pasta.

THAI DRESSING		
Mayonnaise	1/2 cup	125 mL
Chopped fresh cilantro or parsley, lightly packed	1/4 cup	60 mL
Peanut butter	1 tbsp.	15 mL
Rice vinegar	1 tbsp.	15 mL
Soy sauce	1 tbsp.	15 mL
Garlic cloves (or 1/2 tsp., 2 mL, powder)	2	2
Finely grated gingerroot	1 tsp.	5 mL
Granulated sugar	1 tsp.	5 mL
Dried crushed chilies	1/2 tsp.	2 mL

SALAD		
Cut or torn romaine lettuce, lightly packed	6 cups	1.5 L
Chopped cooked chicken (see Coach, page 31)	4 cups	1 L
Dry chow mein noodles	1 cup	250 mL
Fresh bean sprouts	1 cup	250 mL
Grated carrot	1 cup	250 mL
Thinly sliced radish (optional)	1 cup	250 mL

Thai Dressing: Put all 9 ingredients into blender. Process for about 30 seconds until smooth. Makes about 3/4 cup (175 mL) dressing.

Salad: Put all 6 ingredients into large bowl. Drizzle with Thai dressing. Toss. Makes about 10 cups (2.5 L).

1 cup (250 mL): 236 Calories; 13.3 g Total Fat (5.8 g Mono, 4.2 g Poly, 2.2 g Sat); 56 mg Cholesterol; 10 g Carbohydrate; 2 g Fibre; 19 g Protein; 235 mg Sodium

Pictured on page 53.

BLT Salad

A meal salad that tastes just like a BLT sandwich. If you'd like a little more protein, add some chopped cooked chicken, beans or a chopped hard-cooked egg.

Bacon slices, diced	12	12
Iceberg lettuce mix, lightly packed	8 cups	2 L
Coarsely chopped tomato	2 cups	500 mL
Seasoned croutons	1 1/2 cups	375 mL
DRESSING		
Salad dressing (or mayonnaise)	1/2 cup	125 mL
Milk	3 tbsp.	50 mL
Granulated sugar	1/2 tsp.	2 mL
Prepared mustard	1/2 tsp.	2 mL

Cook bacon in large frying pan on medium for 8 to 10 minutes until browned. Transfer with slotted spoon to paper towel-lined plate to drain. Cool.

Meanwhile, put next 3 ingredients into large bowl.

Dressing: Combine all 4 ingredients in small bowl. Add to lettuce mixture. Add bacon. Toss. Makes about 12 cups (3 L).

1 cup (250 mL): 111 Calories; 8.2 g Total Fat (4.3 g Mono, 2.1 g Poly, 1.5 g Sat); 9 mg Cholesterol; 6 g Carbohydrate; 1 g Fibre; 3 g Protein; 246 mg Sodium

Dill Pickle Potato Salad

This can be your signature dish for all your family get-togethers.
The dill flavour makes it out of the ordinary.

Baby potatoes, quartered	1 lb.	454 g
Diced dill pickle	1/2 cup	125 mL
Salad dressing (or mayonnaise)	1/2 cup	125 mL
Green onion, thinly sliced	1	1
Dill pickle juice	1 tbsp.	15 mL
Prepared mustard	1 tsp.	5 mL
Large hard-cooked eggs (see Coach, below), chopped	2	2
Paprika, sprinkle		

Pour water into large saucepan until about 1 inch (2.5 cm) deep. Add potatoes. Cover. Bring to a boil. Reduce heat to medium. Boil gently for 12 to 15 minutes until tender. Drain. Rinse with cold water until cooled. Drain well. Transfer to large bowl.

Combine next 5 ingredients in small bowl. Add egg. Stir. Add to potatoes. Stir until coated.

Sprinkle with paprika. Makes about 3 cups (750 mL).

1 cup (250 mL): 375 Calories; 22.6 g Total Fat (12.1 g Mono, 6.9 g Poly, 2.4 g Sat); 134 mg Cholesterol; 34 g Carbohydrate; 2 g Fibre; 8 g Protein; 717 mg Sodium

COACH

To make hard-cooked eggs, place eggs in a single layer in a saucepan. Add cold water until it's about 1 inch (2.5 cm) above the eggs. Cover. Bring to a boil. Reduce heat to medium-low. Simmer for 10 minutes. Drain. Cover the eggs with cold water. Change the water each time it warms until the eggs are cool enough to handle. Remove the shells. You can do this while the potatoes are cooking to save time.

Salads & Soups

Taco Salad

Honestly, do you know anyone who doesn't like taco salad?
It's a smart pick when you're pressed to create a crowd-pleasing dinner.
You can always omit the onion and garlic if time is of the essence.

Cooking oil	1 tsp.	5 mL
Lean ground beef	1 lb.	454 g
Finely chopped onion	1 cup	250 mL
Garlic cloves, minced	2	2
(or 1/2 tsp., 2 mL, powder)		
Envelope of taco seasoning mix	1 1/4 oz.	35 g
Iceberg lettuce mix, lightly packed	8 cups	2 L
Grated Mexican cheese blend	2 cups	500 mL
Chopped tomato	1 cup	250 mL
Frozen kernel corn, thawed	1 cup	250 mL
Can of sliced black olives, drained	4 1/2 oz.	125 mL
Ranch (or Thousand Island) dressing	1 cup	250 mL
Tortilla chips	4 cups	1 L

Heat cooking oil in large frying pan on medium. Add next 3 ingredients. Scramble-fry for about 10 minutes until beef is no longer pink. Drain.

Add taco seasoning. Heat and stir for 1 minute. Transfer to baking sheet with sides. Spread in thin layer. Chill until cool.

Meanwhile, put next 5 ingredients into large bowl. Toss. Add beef.

Drizzle with dressing. Toss.

Serve with tortilla chips. Serves 4.

1 serving: 1020 Calories; 69.7 g Total Fat (8.7 g Mono, 2.7 g Poly, 22.8 g Sat); 155 mg Cholesterol; 44 g Carbohydrate; 4 g Fibre; 52 g Protein; 2298 mg Sodium

COACH For a fancier presentation, ingredients can be layered in a clear bowl and tossed at the table before serving. Or consider "plating" the salads. This means you make individual salads for everyone, rather than one big one.

Lentil Feta Salad

Although they're teeny tiny, lentils pack a hearty
punch and make this salad quite filling.

Can of lentils, rinsed and drained	19 oz.	540 mL
Chopped green pepper	1/2 cup	125 mL
Chopped red pepper	1/2 cup	125 mL
Chopped tomato	1/2 cup	125 mL
Chopped green onion	1/4 cup	60 mL
Italian dressing	1/4 cup	60 mL
Lemon juice	2 tbsp.	30 mL
Granulated sugar	1 tsp.	5 mL
Pepper	1/4 tsp.	1 mL
Crumbled feta cheese	1 cup	250 mL

Combine first 5 ingredients in medium bowl.

Combine next 4 ingredients in small cup. Drizzle over lentil mixture. Toss until coated.

Sprinkle with feta cheese. Makes about 4 1/2 cups (1.1 L).

1 cup (250 mL): 282 Calories; 16.5 g Total Fat (6.6 g Mono, 3.3 g Poly, 5.8 g Sat);
39 mg Cholesterol; 22 g Carbohydrate; 9 g Fibre; 13 g Protein; 730 mg Sodium

Pictured on page 143 and on back cover.

Hot-And-Sour Slaw

Be the hot topic at the next potluck with this uniquely spicy slaw.

Coleslaw mix	8 cups	2 L
Can of sliced water chestnuts, drained and chopped	8 oz.	227 mL
Thinly sliced red onion	1/2 cup	125 mL
HOT-AND-SOUR DRESSING		
Rice vinegar	1/4 cup	60 mL
Lime juice	2 tbsp.	30 mL
Soy sauce	2 tbsp.	30 mL
Granulated sugar	1 tbsp.	15 mL

(continued on next page)

Garlic clove, minced	1	1
(or 1/4 tsp., 1 mL, powder)		
Dried crushed chilies	1/4 tsp.	1 mL

Put first 3 ingredients into large bowl. Toss.

Hot-And-Sour Dressing: Combine all 6 ingredients in jar with tight-fitting lid. Shake well. Makes about 1/2 cup (125 mL) dressing. Drizzle over salad. Toss. Makes about 8 cups (2 L).

1 cup (250 mL): 55 Calories; 0.3 g Total Fat (trace Mono, 0.1 g Poly, trace Sat); 0 mg Cholesterol; 13 g Carbohydrate; 4 g Fibre; 2 g Protein; 233 mg Sodium

---

Spinach Pesto Salad

*The bold basil-scented vinaigrette adds a refreshing flair
to this spinach salad loaded with pine nuts and sweet tomatoes.*

PESTO VINAIGRETTE

Basil pesto	3 tbsp.	50 mL
Apple cider vinegar	2 tbsp.	30 mL
Olive (or cooking) oil	2 tbsp.	30 mL
Grated lemon zest	1 tsp.	5 mL
Salt	1/8 tsp.	0.5 mL

SALAD

Fresh spinach leaves, lightly packed	6 cups	1.5 L
Grape tomatoes	1 cup	250 mL
Pine nuts, toasted (see Coach, page 63)	2/3 cup	150 mL

Pesto Vinaigrette: Combine all 5 ingredients in jar with tight-fitting lid. Shake well. Makes about 1/2 cup (125 mL) vinaigrette.

Salad: Put all 3 ingredients into large bowl. Drizzle with Pesto Vinaigrette. Toss. Makes about 6 cups (1.5 L).

1 cup (250 mL): 179 Calories; 16.2 g Total Fat (7.4 g Mono, 5.3 g Poly, 2.4 g Sat); trace Cholesterol; 6 g Carbohydrate; 4 g Fibre; 6 g Protein; 159 mg Sodium

Pictured on page 53.

Chicken Salad Fiesta

A bean salad with a spicy zing. If you want to up the crunch factor,
serve on a bed of crisp lettuce.

Chopped cooked chicken	3 cups	750 mL
(see Coach, page 31)		
Canned black beans, rinsed and drained	1 cup	250 mL
Frozen kernel corn, thawed	1 cup	250 mL
Chopped red pepper	1/2 cup	125 mL
Grated lime zest	1 tsp.	5 mL
Salsa	1 cup	250 mL
Ketchup	1 tbsp.	15 mL
Lime juice	1 tbsp.	15 mL
Olive (or cooking) oil	1 tbsp.	15 mL
Garlic clove, minced	1	1
(or 1/4 tsp., 1 mL, powder)		
Salt	1/4 tsp.	1 mL
Drops of hot pepper sauce	4	4

Chopped fresh parsley, for garnish

Combine first 5 ingredients in large bowl.

Combine next 7 ingredients in small bowl. Add to chicken mixture.
Toss until coated.

Sprinkle with parsley. Makes about 5 cups (1.25 L).

1 cup (250 mL): 284 Calories; 10.7 g Total Fat (4.8 g Mono, 2.1 g Poly, 2.5 g Sat);
79 mg Cholesterol; 19 g Carbohydrate; 4 g Fibre; 29 g Protein; 667 mg Sodium

1. Spinach Pesto Salad, page 51
2. Thai Chicken Salad, page 46
3. White Bean Soup, page 56

Props courtesy of: Casa Bugatti
Pier 1 Imports
Stokes

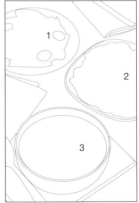

Simple Salad

Sometimes you just want a good ol' green salad.
The vinaigrette makes it special.

Mixed salad greens, lightly packed	8 cups	2 L
Sliced red pepper	1 1/2 cups	375 mL
Chopped walnuts, toasted	1/3 cup	75 mL
(see Coach, page 63)		
Raisins	1/3 cup	75 mL
Sliced red onion	1/4 cup	60 mL
SIMPLE DRESSING		
Olive (or cooking) oil	1/4 cup	60 mL
White vinegar	2 tbsp.	30 mL
Granulated sugar	2 tsp.	10 mL
Dry mustard	1/2 tsp.	2 mL
Salt	1/8 tsp.	0.5 mL

Put first 5 ingredients into large bowl. Toss.

Simple Dressing: Combine all 5 ingredients in jar with tight-fitting lid. Shake well. Makes about 1/3 cup (75 mL) dressing. Drizzle over lettuce mixture. Toss until coated. Makes about 9 cups (2.25 L).

1 cup (250 mL): 121 Calories; 9.1 g Total Fat (4.8 g Mono, 2.7 g Poly, 1.1 g Sat); 0 mg Cholesterol; 10 g Carbohydrate; 2 g Fibre; 2 g Protein; 53 mg Sodium

Pictured on page 54.

1. Italian Garlic Bread, page 76
2. Simple Salad, above
3. Chicken Picadillo, page 102

Props courtesy of: Pier 1 Imports
Danesco Inc.

White Bean Soup

Feel like you've "bean there, done that?" Try this bean soup with a difference. The fresh flavours of green onion and tomato are showcased in this spicy purée. Use double the amount of chilies if you love spicy food.

Bacon slices, diced	4	4
Chopped onion	1 cup	250 mL
Sliced celery	3/4 cup	175 mL
Bay leaf	1	1
Dried crushed chilies	1/4 tsp.	1 mL
Pepper	1/4 tsp.	1 mL
Prepared chicken broth	4 cups	1 L
Can of navy (or white kidney) beans, rinsed and drained	19 oz.	540 mL
Finely chopped Roma (plum) tomato	3/4 cup	175 mL
Chopped green onion	2 tbsp.	30 mL

Cook bacon in large saucepan on medium-high until crisp. Transfer with slotted spoon to paper towel-lined plate to drain.

Heat 1 tbsp. (15 mL) drippings in same saucepan on medium. Add next 5 ingredients. Cook, uncovered, for about 5 minutes, stirring often (see Note), until onion is softened.

Add broth and beans. Bring to a boil. Reduce heat to medium. Boil gently, uncovered, for 5 minutes to blend flavours. Remove from heat. Discard bay leaf. Carefully process with hand blender or in blender until smooth (see Safety Tip).

Add tomato, green onion and bacon. Stir. Makes about 6 cups (1.5 L).

1 cup (250 mL): 169 Calories; 4.4 g Total Fat (1.9 g Mono, 0.8 g Poly, 1.4 g Sat); 6 mg Cholesterol; 24 g Carbohydrate; 6 g Fibre; 10 g Protein; 1500 mg Sodium

Pictured on page 53.

Note: While stirring, be careful not to break up the bay leaf.

Safety Tip: Follow blender manufacturer's instructions for processing hot liquids.

To make this soup even faster, use 2 tbsp. (30 mL) bacon bits and 1 tbsp. (15 mL) cooking oil instead of bacon and drippings.

Salads & Soups

Dill-icious Spring Soup

Enjoy the colours and flavours of spring any time of year. If you process the hot soup in your blender, be sure to hold a tea towel over the lid while blending.

Butter (or hard margarine)	2 tbsp.	30 mL
Finely chopped onion	1/2 cup	125 mL
Garlic clove, minced	1	1
(or 1/4 tsp., 1 mL, powder)		
All-purpose flour	2 tbsp.	30 mL
Prepared chicken broth	3 cups	750 mL
Chopped fresh asparagus	1 1/2 cups	375 mL
Frozen peas	1 cup	250 mL
Grated lemon zest	2 tsp.	10 mL
Bay leaf	1	1
Seasoned salt	1/2 tsp.	2 mL
Half-and-half cream	1/2 cup	125 mL
Chopped fresh dill (or 1 tbsp., 15 mL, dried)	1/4 cup	60 mL

Melt butter in large saucepan on medium-high. Add onion and garlic. Cook for about 2 minutes, stirring often, until onion is softened.

Sprinkle with flour. Heat and stir for 1 minute.

Slowly add 1 cup (250 mL) broth. Heat and stir until boiling and thickened. Add remaining broth and next 5 ingredients. Stir. Reduce heat to medium-low. Simmer, covered, for about 5 minutes, stirring occasionally, until asparagus is tender. Discard bay leaf.

Add cream and dill. Cook and stir for about 1 minute until heated through. Carefully process with hand blender or in blender until smooth (see Safety Tip). Makes about 5 cups (1.25 L).

1 cup (250 mL): 201 Calories; 8.2 g Total Fat (2.3 g Mono, 0.6 g Poly, 4.9 g Sat); 21 mg Cholesterol; 22 g Carbohydrate; 8 g Fibre; 10 g Protein; 1105 mg Sodium

Safety Tip: Follow blender manufacturer's instructions for processing hot liquids.

COACH

Soups that don't have pasta or potatoes in them are great for freezing. Make double the batch and freeze in individual containers for lunches. If the soup has milk or cream in it, expect it to separate after freezing. Just whisk it up while heating and it will be as good as new.

Ginger Carrot Soup

*Think carrot soup is rabbit feed? No way! This vibrant,
smooth soup packs one heck of a gingery punch.*

Cooking oil	1/2 tsp.	2 mL
Frozen sliced carrots	4 cups	1 L
Chopped onion	1 cup	250 mL
Finely grated gingerroot	1 tsp.	5 mL
(or 1/4 tsp., 1 mL, ground ginger)		
Prepared chicken broth	4 cups	1 L
Curry powder	1/4 tsp.	1 mL
Garlic powder	1/4 tsp.	1 mL
Salt	1/2 tsp.	2 mL
Pepper	1/8 tsp.	0.5 mL
Evaporated milk (or half-and-half cream)	1 cup	250 mL

Heat cooking oil in large saucepan on medium-high. Add carrot and onion.
Cook for about 5 minutes, stirring often, until onion starts to soften.

Add ginger. Stir.

Add next 5 ingredients. Stir. Bring to a boil. Reduce heat to medium.
Boil gently, covered, for about 15 minutes until carrot is tender.
Remove from heat.

Add evaporated milk. Stir. Carefully process with hand blender or in
blender until smooth (see Safety Tip). Makes about 8 cups (2 L) of super
soup for you and your lucky friends.

*1 cup (250 mL): 77 Calories; 1.6 g Total Fat (0.6 g Mono, 0.4 g Poly, 0.6 g Sat);
2 mg Cholesterol; 12 g Carbohydrate; 2 g Fibre; 4 g Protein; 961 mg Sodium*

Safety Tip: Follow blender manufacturer's instructions for processing
hot liquids.

Lots of people peel gingerroot with a vegetable peeler—
this works but it does create a lot of waste. Because the skin on
the ginger is so thin, you can actually peel it off by scraping it
with the edge of a spoon—it comes off very easily.

Quick Tomato Soup

Consider this your most basic soup recipe.

Cooking oil	1 tsp.	5 mL
Chopped onion	1 cup	250 mL
Can of diced tomatoes (with juice)	28 oz.	796 mL
Prepared chicken (or vegetable) broth	2 cups	500 mL
Can of tomato sauce	7 1/2 oz.	213 mL
Whipping cream	1/2 cup	125 mL
Chopped fresh basil	2 tbsp.	30 mL

Heat cooking oil in large saucepan on medium. Add onion. Cook, uncovered, for 5 to 10 minutes, stirring often, until softened.

Add next 3 ingredients. Stir. Bring to a boil. Reduce heat to medium-low. Simmer, partially covered, for 5 minutes to blend flavours.

Add cream and basil. Stir. Carefully process with hand blender or in blender until smooth (see Safety Tip). Makes about 6 cups (1.5 L).

1 cup (250 mL): 123 Calories; 8.2 g Total Fat (2.6 g Mono, 0.6 g Poly, 4.5 g Sat); 25 mg Cholesterol; 12 g Carbohydrate; 1 g Fibre; 3 g Protein; 1078 mg Sodium

Safety Tip: Follow blender manufacturer's instructions for processing hot liquids.

Spicy Gazpacho

This chilled soup is quick, spicy, healthy and brilliantly coloured.

Tomato juice	2 cups	500 mL
Finely chopped English cucumber (with peel)	1 cup	250 mL
Finely chopped Roma (plum) tomato	1 cup	250 mL
Finely chopped onion	1/2 cup	125 mL
Finely chopped yellow pepper	1/2 cup	125 mL
Lime juice	2 tbsp.	30 mL
Granulated sugar	2 tsp.	10 mL
Chili paste (sambal oelek)	1 tsp.	5 mL
Salt	1/2 tsp.	2 mL
Pepper	1/2 tsp.	2 mL

Combine all 10 ingredients in large bowl. Ladle half of vegetable mixture into blender. Process until almost smooth. Return to same bowl. Stir. Makes about 4 cups (1 L).

1 cup (250 mL): 59 Calories; 0.3 g Total Fat (0.1 g Mono, 0.1 g Poly, 0.1 g Sat); 0 mg Cholesterol; 14 g Carbohydrate; 2 g Fibre; 2 g Protein; 763 mg Sodium

Spicy Potato Wedges

Live life on the wedge! These spicy fries are a great alternative to deep-fried potatoes—they're less messy and more healthy to boot.

Large unpeeled potatoes	2	2
Cooking oil	1 tbsp.	15 mL
Montreal steak spice	1 tbsp.	15 mL

Preheat oven to 425°F (220°C). Prick potatoes in several places with fork. Wrap individually with paper towel. Microwave on high (100%) for 8 to 10 minutes, turning at halftime, until tender. Let stand for about 3 minutes until cool enough to handle. Cut potatoes lengthwise into 8 wedges each. Transfer to medium bowl.

Add cooking oil. Toss until coated. Arrange wedges on greased baking sheet with sides.

Sprinkle steak spice over top. Bake for about 10 minutes until heated through. Makes 16 wedges.

1 wedge: 43 Calories; 0.9 g Total Fat (0.5 g Mono, 0.3 g Poly, 0.1 g Sat); 0 mg Cholesterol; 8 g Carbohydrate; 1 g Fibre; 1 g Protein; 95 mg Sodium

Sun-Dried Tomato Asparagus

Even though it's a vegetable, many people think asparagus is a real treat— especially when it's dressed up with tangy balsamic vinegar and flavourful pesto.

Fresh asparagus, trimmed of tough ends	1 lb.	454 g
Salt	1/2 tsp.	2 mL
Balsamic vinegar	2 tbsp.	30 mL
Olive (or cooking) oil	1 tbsp.	15 mL
Sun-dried tomato pesto	1 tbsp.	15 mL
Grated lemon zest	1/2 tsp.	2 mL
Grated Parmesan cheese	2 tbsp.	30 mL

Pour water into large frying pan until about 1 inch (2.5 cm) deep. Add asparagus and salt. Bring to a boil. Reduce heat to medium. Boil gently for about 4 minutes until tender-crisp. Drain. Transfer to serving plate.

Meanwhile, combine next 4 ingredients in small cup. Drizzle over asparagus.

(continued on next page)

Sprinkle cheese over top. Serves 4.

1 serving: 137 Calories; 7.9 g Total Fat (3.9 g Mono, 0.4 g Poly, 3.4 g Sat); 12 mg Cholesterol; 7 g Carbohydrate; 3 g Fibre; 9 g Protein; 324 mg Sodium

To trim asparagus ends, just use kitchen scissors and snip at the point where the stalk starts to become pliable.

Snap-To-Attention Peas And Carrots

Get snap pea happy! This more elegant version of peas and carrots has a buttery, seasoned coating.

Butter (or hard margarine)	3 tbsp.	50 mL
Sugar snap peas, trimmed	4 cups	1 L
Thinly sliced carrot	1 cup	250 mL
Dijon mustard	2 tsp.	10 mL
Balsamic vinegar	1 tsp.	5 mL
Lemon pepper	1 tsp.	5 mL
Liquid honey	1 tsp.	5 mL

Melt butter in large frying pan on medium. Add peas and carrot. Stir-fry for 3 to 5 minutes until vegetables are tender-crisp.

Combine remaining 4 ingredients in small cup. Add to vegetable mixture. Toss until coated. Makes about 4 cups (1 L).

1 cup (250 mL): 142 Calories; 8.6 g Total Fat (2.2 g Mono, 0.4 g Poly, 5.4 g Sat); 23 mg Cholesterol; 13 g Carbohydrate; 4 g Fibre; 3 g Protein; 195 mg Sodium

Invest in a pair of kitchen scissors to make quick work of trimming the ends of sugar snap peas, and cutting all manner of things. They come in super handy. Wash them by hand or just put them in the dishwasher.

Half-Baked,
Completely-Good Potatoes

Baby potatoes are all grown-up with a dusting of oregano and Parmesan.
These are a great match with an oven-roasted main dish. If you can't get baby
potatoes, just cut four large baking potatoes into eighths.

Baby potatoes, larger ones cut in half	2 lbs.	900 g
Olive (or cooking) oil	2 tbsp.	30 mL
Grated Parmesan cheese	1/4 cup	60 mL
Dried oregano	1 tsp.	5 mL
Seasoned salt	1/2 tsp.	2 mL
Pepper	1/4 tsp.	1 mL

Preheat oven to 450°F (230°C). Put potatoes into large microwave-safe bowl. Microwave, covered, on high (100%) for about 8 minutes until almost tender. Drizzle with olive oil. Toss until coated.

Meanwhile, combine remaining 4 ingredients in small bowl. Add to potatoes. Toss until coated. Transfer to greased baking sheet with sides. Spread evenly. Bake for about 10 minutes until potatoes are tender. Makes about 5 cups (1.25 L).

1 cup (250 mL): 309 Calories; 12.7 g Total Fat (6.3 g Mono, 0.6 g Poly, 5.4 g Sat);
19 mg Cholesterol; 33 g Carbohydrate; 2 g Fibre; 14 g Protein; 603 mg Sodium

Sesame Baby Bok Choy

There's no need to be a microwave snob when you can make great dishes like this unique, Asian-flavoured bok choy side. The microwave is the busy chef's best friend. Veggies are great cooked in the microwave—they retain their color and, as long as they're not overcooked, their crispness.

Whole baby bok choy, halved	4	4
Prepared chicken (or vegetable) broth	1/4 cup	60 mL
Hoisin sauce	1 tbsp.	15 mL
Cooking oil	1 tsp.	5 mL
Sweet chili sauce	1 tsp.	5 mL
Finely grated gingerroot	1/2 tsp.	2 mL
(or 1/8 tsp., 0.5 mL, ground ginger)		
Sesame seeds, toasted (see Coach, below)	2 tsp.	10 mL

Arrange bok choy in circle on large microwave-safe plate, with leaf ends toward centre of plate.

Combine next 5 ingredients in small cup. Pour over bok choy. Microwave, covered, on high (100%) for about 5 minutes until tender-crisp. Let stand, covered, for 30 seconds.

Sprinkle sesame seeds over top. Serves 4.

1 serving: 43 Calories; 2.3 g Total Fat (1.0 g Mono, 0.9 g Poly, 0.3 g Sat); trace Cholesterol; 5 g Carbohydrate; 1 g Fibre; 2 g Protein; 224 mg Sodium

When toasting nuts, seeds or coconut, cooking times will vary for each type of nut—so never toast them together. For small amounts, place ingredient in an ungreased shallow frying pan. Heat on medium for 3 to 5 minutes, stirring often, until golden. For larger amounts, spread ingredient evenly in an ungreased shallow pan. Bake in a 350°F (175°C) oven for 5 to 10 minutes, stirring or shaking often, until golden.

Curry Their Favour Rice

A curry side will spice up any main dish. The bright green peas and crunchy toasted almonds make this side a wonderful complement to grilled meats.

Cooking oil	1 tbsp.	15 mL
Finely chopped onion	1/2 cup	125 mL
Grated peeled cooking apple	1/2 cup	125 mL
(such as McIntosh)		
Curry powder	1 tsp.	5 mL
Ground nutmeg, sprinkle		
Prepared chicken broth	2 cups	500 mL
Long grain white rice	1 cup	250 mL
Frozen peas	1/2 cup	125 mL
Sliced almonds, toasted (see Coach, page 63)	1/4 cup	60 mL

Heat cooking oil in medium saucepan on medium-high. Add next 4 ingredients. Cook for 2 to 4 minutes, stirring often, until onion is softened.

Add broth. Stir. Bring to a boil. Reduce heat to medium-low. Add rice. Stir. Simmer, covered, for 15 minutes, without stirring.

Add peas. Stir. Simmer, covered, for about 5 minutes, without stirring, until liquid is absorbed and rice is tender. Fluff with fork.

Sprinkle almonds over top. Makes about 3 1/2 cups (875 mL).

1 cup (250 mL): 390 Calories; 13.5 g Total Fat (8.1 g Mono, 3.3 g Poly, 1.4 g Sat); 0 mg Cholesterol; 58 g Carbohydrate; 2 g Fibre; 10 g Protein; 875 mg Sodium

Glazed Dill Carrots

Here's an easy way to make a simple side impressive.

Baby carrots, halved crosswise	3 cups	750 mL
Liquid honey	1/4 cup	60 mL
Butter (or hard margarine)	2 tbsp.	30 mL
Dried dillweed	1/2 tsp.	2 mL

(continued on next page)

Pour water into large saucepan until about 1 inch (2.5 cm) deep. Add carrots. Cover. Bring to a boil. Reduce heat to medium. Boil gently for 8 to 10 minutes until carrots are tender-crisp. Drain.

Add remaining 3 ingredients. Heat and stir until butter is melted and carrots are coated. Makes about 3 cups (750 mL).

1 cup (250 mL): 245 Calories; 8.8 g Total Fat (2.0 g Mono, 0.9 g Poly, 5.0 g Sat); 20 mg Cholesterol; 42 g Carbohydrate; 4 g Fibre; 2 g Protein; 135 mg Sodium

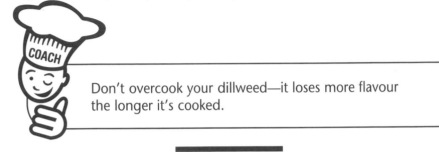

Don't overcook your dillweed—it loses more flavour the longer it's cooked.

Champ

This Irish-inspired spin on mashed potatoes is so simple, yet so good!

Cubed peeled potato	6 cups	1.5 L
Hot milk	1 cup	250 mL
Green onions, chopped	6	6
Butter (or hard margarine)	1/4 cup	60 mL
Salt	1 tsp.	5 mL
Pepper	1/2 tsp.	2 mL

Pour water into medium saucepan until about 1 inch (2.5 cm) deep. Add potato. Cover. Bring to a boil. Reduce heat to medium. Boil gently for 12 to 15 minutes until tender. Drain. Mash.

Add remaining 5 ingredients. Mash. Makes about 6 cups (1.5 L)—enough to satisfy all the potato lovers you know.

1 cup (250 mL): 228 Calories; 8.2 g Total Fat (2.1 g Mono, 0.4 g Poly, 5.1 g Sat); 23 mg Cholesterol; 35 g Carbohydrate; 3 g Fibre; 5 g Protein; 477 mg Sodium

BAKED POTATO CHAMP: Use 1 cup (250 mL) hot sour cream and 3 tbsp. (50 mL) chopped fresh chives instead of milk and green onion. Add 3 tbsp. (50 mL) bacon bits.

SOUTHWESTERN CHAMP: Use 1 cup (250 mL) hot buttermilk instead of milk and butter. Omit green onion. Add 1/4 cup (60 mL) salsa, 1 tbsp. (15 mL) minced chipotle pepper in adobo sauce and 1 minced garlic clove (or 1/4 tsp., 1 mL, powder).

Sweet Potato Couscous

This curried couscous with tender sweet potatoes and crunchy almonds makes a perfect side for grilled meats. This dish is designed to be served warm, but if you like it hot (some do, we hear), then heat it in the microwave until the sweet potato is hot.

Prepared vegetable broth	1 1/4 cups	300 mL
Butter (or hard margarine)	2 tbsp.	30 mL
Honey	1 tbsp.	15 mL
Curry powder	1 tsp.	5 mL
Pepper	1/4 tsp.	1 mL
Couscous	1 1/4 cups	300 mL
Frozen peas	1/2 cup	125 mL
Can of sweet potatoes, drained and cut into bite-sized pieces	19 oz.	540 mL
Slivered almonds	1/4 cup	60 mL
Sliced green onion	2 tbsp.	30 mL

Combine first 5 ingredients in large saucepan. Bring to a boil.

Add couscous and peas. Stir. Remove from heat. Let stand, covered, for 5 minutes. Fluff with fork.

Add remaining 3 ingredients. Stir. Makes about 6 cups (1.5 L).

1 cup (250 mL): 321 Calories; 7.5 g Total Fat (3.0 g Mono, 1.1 g Poly, 2.7 g Sat); 10 mg Cholesterol; 56 g Carbohydrate; 5 g Fibre; 8 g Protein; 171 mg Sodium

Braised Red Cabbage

This uncommon side will impress any gourmet guest with its sweet taste, cranberry tang and vibrant colour.

Butter (or hard margarine)	2 tbsp.	30 mL
Chopped red cabbage	4 cups	1 L
Chopped onion	1 cup	250 mL
Apple juice	1/2 cup	125 mL
Dried cranberries	1/2 cup	125 mL
Apple cider vinegar	2 tbsp.	30 mL
Brown sugar, packed	2 tbsp.	30 mL
Salt	1/2 tsp.	2 mL
Pepper	1/4 tsp.	1 mL

Heat butter in large frying pan on medium until melted and bubbles have disappeared. Add cabbage and onion. Cook for about 5 minutes, stirring occasionally, until cabbage starts to soften and lighten in colour. Reduce heat to medium-low.

Add remaining 6 ingredients. Stir. Cook, covered, for about 15 minutes until cabbage is tender-crisp. Makes about 4 cups (1 L).

1 cup (250 mL): 173 Calories; 5.9 g Total Fat (1.5 g Mono, 0.3 g Poly, 3.6 g Sat); 15 mg Cholesterol; 32 g Carbohydrate; 3 g Fibre; 1 g Protein; 346 mg Sodium

Pictured on page 71.

Red cabbage can make a colourful addition to an otherwise neutral meal but if you want its colour to pop, there are a few things you need to keep in mind:

- Always cook it with a little bit of acidic liquid (like vinegar).
- Don't cook it in aluminum cookware.
- Don't cut it with a carbon-steel knife.

Lemon Cranberry Couscous

The tart taste of cranberry adds a real nice zing to anything it's in. Pair this side with roast chicken or pork to get the biggest bang out of your berries.

Prepared chicken broth	3 cups	750 mL
Lemon juice	2 tbsp.	30 mL
Grated lemon zest (see Coach, page 80)	2 tsp.	10 mL
Box of plain couscous	12 oz.	340 g
Dried cranberries	2/3 cup	150 mL
Olive (or cooking) oil	2 tsp.	10 mL
Chopped fresh parsley	2 tbsp.	30 mL

Combine first 3 ingredients in large saucepan. Bring to a boil.

Add next 3 ingredients. Stir. Remove from heat. Let stand, covered, for 5 minutes. Fluff with fork.

Sprinkle parsley over top. Makes about 5 3/4 cups (1.45 L).

1 cup (250 mL): 292 Calories; 2.5 g Total Fat (1.4 g Mono, 0.5 g Poly, 0.4 g Sat); 0 mg Cholesterol; 59 g Carbohydrate; 3 g Fibre; 8 g Protein; 781 mg Sodium

Pictured on page 71.

Sesame Ginger Chickpeas

Chickpeas on their own are pretty boring but their subtle taste makes them a great medium to showcase more vibrant flavours. Serve this Asian-inspired side with chicken or pork.

Cooking oil	1 tsp.	5 mL
Chopped celery	1 cup	250 mL
Chopped onion	1 cup	250 mL
Can of chickpeas (garbanzo beans), rinsed and drained	19 oz.	540 mL
Chopped red pepper	1 cup	250 mL
Sesame ginger dressing	1/3 cup	75 mL
Chopped fresh parsley	1 tbsp.	15 mL

(continued on next page)

Sides

Heat cooking oil in medium saucepan on medium. Add celery and onion. Cook for about 5 minutes, stirring often, until onion starts to soften.

Add next 3 ingredients. Stir. Cook, covered, for 3 to 5 minutes until heated through.

Sprinkle parsley over top. Makes about 3 1/2 cups (875 mL).

1 cup (250 mL): 268 Calories; 11.9 g Total Fat (1.4 g Mono, 1.7 g Poly, 1.2 g Sat); 0 mg Cholesterol; 34 g Carbohydrate; 8 g Fibre; 9 g Protein; 386 mg Sodium

Bacon Garlic Green Beans

Bacon adds a wonderful smoky flavour to almost any veggie. If you're in a rush or just plain out of bacon, use real bacon bits instead— just add them with the basil.

Bacon slices, diced	2	2
Fresh (or frozen, thawed) whole green beans	4 cups	1 L
Prepared chicken broth	1/4 cup	60 mL
Garlic clove, minced	1	1
(or 1/4 tsp., 1 mL, powder)		
Chopped fresh basil	1 tbsp.	15 mL

Cook bacon in large frying pan on medium-high for about 3 minutes until starting to brown.

Add next 3 ingredients. Stir. Reduce heat to medium. Cook, covered, for 5 to 6 minutes, stirring at halftime, until green beans are tender-crisp.

Add basil. Toss. Makes about 4 cups (1 L).

1 cup (250 mL): 115 Calories; 5.7 g Total Fat (3.6 g Mono, 1.0 g Poly, 3.1 g Sat); 8 mg Cholesterol; 14 g Carbohydrate; 5 g Fibre; 5 g Protein; 168 mg Sodium

COACH

Recipes rarely call for a whole package of bacon, so it's wise to separate a package into smaller bundles of two or three strips each. Just wrap the bundles well in plastic wrap and put them in the freezer.

Orange Teriyaki Stir-Fry

*Serve your nearest and dearest this citrusy stir-fry and they'll be (teri)yakkin'
about it for days to come. And with frozen veggies you still get all of the flavour
and nutrition and none of the chopping, slicing and peeling.*

Soy sauce	2 tbsp.	30 mL
Cornstarch	1 tsp.	5 mL
Orange juice	1/2 cup	125 mL
Brown sugar, packed	1 tbsp.	15 mL
Chili sauce	2 tsp.	10 mL
Finely grated gingerroot	2 tsp.	10 mL
(or 1/2 tsp., 2 mL, ground ginger)		
Garlic cloves, minced	2	2
(or 1/2 tsp., 2 mL, powder)		
Grated orange zest	1 tsp.	5 mL
Hoisin sauce	1 tsp.	5 mL
Cooking oil	1 tsp.	5 mL
Frozen Oriental mixed vegetables	6 cups	1.5 L

Stir soy sauce into cornstarch in small bowl. Add next 7 ingredients. Stir well.

Heat large frying pan or wok on medium-high until very hot. Add cooking
oil. Add vegetables. Stir-fry for 2 minutes. Stir cornstarch mixture. Add
to vegetable mixture. Stir. Cook, covered, for 4 to 5 minutes until
vegetables are tender-crisp and sauce is boiling and thickened. Makes
about 3 cups (750 mL).

*1 cup (250 mL): 232 Calories; 4.7 g Total Fat (0.9 g Mono, 0.5 g Poly, 0.7 g Sat); 1 mg Cholesterol;
38 g Carbohydrate; 2 g Fibre; 8 g Protein; 1682 mg Sodium*

Pictured on page 71.

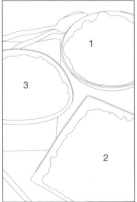

1. Orange Teriyaki Stir-Fry, above
2. Lemon Cranberry Couscous, page 68
3. Braised Red Cabbage, page 67

Props courtesy of: The Bay
Winners Stores

Sides

Cucumber Chutney

Fruit + curry + cucumber = delicious! The flavours are even more intense the second day. Best served with grilled pork or chicken.

Cooking oil	1/2 tsp.	2 mL
Chopped onion	1 cup	250 mL
Chopped red pepper	1 cup	250 mL
Chopped dried apricot	1/4 cup	60 mL
Apple juice	1/2 cup	125 mL
Dried cranberries	1/2 cup	125 mL
Curry powder	1 tsp.	5 mL
Garlic powder	1/4 tsp.	1 mL
Ground cumin	1/4 tsp.	1 mL
Salt	1/4 tsp.	1 mL
Pepper	1/8 tsp.	0.5 mL
Diced peeled English cucumber	1 1/3 cups	325 mL

Heat cooking oil in small saucepan on medium. Add onion and red pepper. Cook for about 5 minutes, stirring often, until onion starts to soften.

Add next 8 ingredients. Stir. Simmer, uncovered, for about 5 minutes until liquid is evaporated. Transfer to small bowl.

Add cucumber. Stir. Makes about 3 cups (750 mL).

1/4 cup (60 mL): 40 Calories; 0.3 g Total Fat (0.1 g Mono, 0.1 g Poly, trace Sat); 0 mg Cholesterol; 10 g Carbohydrate; 1 g Fibre; trace Protein; 52 mg Sodium

Pictured on page 72.

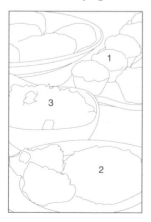

1. Feta Polenta Muffins, page 74
2. Chili Biscuit Flower, page 75
3. Cucumber Chutney, above

Props courtesy of: Pier 1 Imports

Go-Withs

Feta Polenta Muffins

Although this recipe doesn't use polenta, per se, the cornmeal and creamed corn combine for a perfect polenta flavour in this compact muffin. Serve with Chic Chicken Chili, page 106, or Chicken Mole, page 101.

All-purpose flour	1 cup	250 mL
Yellow cornmeal	1 cup	250 mL
Baking soda	1 tsp.	5 mL
Dried basil	1 tsp.	5 mL
Salt	1/4 tsp.	1 mL
Pepper	1/2 tsp.	2 mL
Large eggs, fork-beaten	2	2
Can of cream-style corn	10 oz.	284 mL
Buttermilk (or soured milk, see Coach, page 42)	1/2 cup	125 mL
Cooking oil	2 tbsp.	30 mL
Hot pepper sauce	1/4 tsp.	1 mL
Can of sliced black olives, drained and chopped	4 1/2 oz.	125 mL
Crumbled feta cheese	1/2 cup	125 mL

Preheat oven to 400°F (205°C). Measure first 6 ingredients into large bowl. Stir. Make a well in centre.

Combine next 5 ingredients in medium bowl. Add to well.

Add olives and feta. Stir until just moistened. Divide batter into 24 greased mini-muffin cups. Bake for about 15 minutes until wooden pick inserted in centre of muffin comes out clean. Let stand in pan for 5 minutes. Remove muffins from pan and place on wire rack to cool. Makes 24 mini-muffins.

1 mini-muffin: 77 Calories; 2.8 g Total Fat (1.3 g Mono, 0.5 g Poly, 0.8 g Sat); 19 mg Cholesterol; 11 g Carbohydrate; 1 g Fibre; 2 g Protein; 187 mg Sodium

Pictured on page 72.

Chili Biscuit Flower

Giving flowers is always a great way to brighten someone's day.
This flower, although not your typical flora, is sure to put a smile on anyone's
face. Think of it as flower power. Serve with soups, chilies and salads.

Tube of refrigerator country-style biscuits (10 biscuits per tube)	12 oz.	340 g
Butter (or hard margarine), melted	1 tbsp.	15 mL
Chili powder	1/4 tsp.	1 mL
Ground cumin	1/8 tsp.	0.5 mL
Grated Mexican cheese blend	1/2 cup	125 mL
Finely chopped fresh jalapeño pepper (see Coach, below)	2 tbsp.	30 mL

Preheat oven to 400°F (205°C). Separate dough into 10 biscuits. Place 1 biscuit in centre of greased 12 inch (30 cm) pizza pan. Arrange remaining biscuits in circle around centre biscuit, with edges touching. Gently press edges together and press biscuits out to 10 inch (25 cm) circle.

Combine next 3 ingredients in small cup. Brush over biscuits.

Sprinkle with cheese and jalapeño pepper. Bake for about 12 minutes until golden. Makes 10 biscuits.

1 biscuit: 122 Calories; 4.9 g Total Fat (1.3 g Mono, 0.4 g Poly, 2.4 g Sat); 8 mg Cholesterol; 16 g Carbohydrate; trace Fibre; 3 g Protein; 277 mg Sodium

Pictured on page 72.

COACH

Hot peppers contain capsaicin in the seeds and ribs. Removing the seeds and ribs will reduce the heat. Wear rubber gloves when handling hot peppers and avoid touching your eyes. Wash your hands well afterwards.

Italian Garlic Bread

Just a few ordinary ingredients combine to make
top-notch garlic bread. Serve with pasta.

Butter (or hard margarine), softened	6 tbsp.	100 mL
Grated Parmesan cheese	1/4 cup	60 mL
Garlic cloves, minced	2	2
(or 1/2 tsp., 2 mL, powder)		
Italian seasoning	2 tsp.	10 mL
Italian (or French) bread loaf, halved horizontally	1	1

Preheat oven to 400°F (205°C). Combine first 4 ingredients in small bowl.

Spread butter mixture on cut sides of bread. Place, cut-side up, on ungreased baking sheet. Bake for about 15 minutes until heated through and toasted. Each half cuts into 16 pieces, for a total of 32 pieces.

1 piece: 40 Calories; 3.3 g Total Fat (0.9 g Mono, 0.1 g Poly, 2.1 g Sat); 9 mg Cholesterol; 1 g Carbohydrate; trace Fibre; 2 g Protein; 93 mg Sodium

Pictured on page 54.

No-Salt Barbecue Spice

This versatile seasoning mix can be used on chicken, pork or beef.
Store in an airtight container for up to three months.

Brown sugar, packed	1 tbsp.	15 mL
Chili powder	2 tsp.	10 mL
Garlic powder	2 tsp.	10 mL
Paprika	2 tsp.	10 mL
Parsley flakes	2 tsp.	10 mL
Dried basil	1 tsp.	5 mL
Dried marjoram	1 tsp.	5 mL
Pepper	1 tsp.	5 mL

Combine all 8 ingredients in small bowl. Makes about 1/3 cup (75 mL).

1 tsp. (5 mL): 7 Calories; 0.1 g Total Fat (trace Mono, 0.1 g Poly, trace Sat); 0 mg Cholesterol; 2 g Carbohydrate; trace Fibre; trace Protein; 4 mg Sodium

Go-Withs

Tortilla Pesto Flutes

These flavourful tortillas will be music to your mouth. Serve with soup or salad.

Sun-dried tomato pesto	16 tsp.	80 mL
Flour tortillas (6 inch, 15 cm, diameter)	8	8
Chopped fresh basil	3 tbsp.	50 mL
Cooking spray		

Preheat oven to 350°F (175°C). Spread 2 tsp. (10 mL) pesto evenly over each tortilla, almost to edge. Sprinkle basil over top. Roll up tortillas, jelly-roll style. Place, seam-side down, on greased baking sheet with sides.

Spray tortillas with cooking spray. Bake for about 10 minutes until lightly browned and crisp. Makes 8 flutes.

1 flute: 100 Calories; 2.1 g Total Fat (1.1 g Mono, 0.3 g Poly, 0.5 g Sat); 0 mg Cholesterol; 17 g Carbohydrate; 1 g Fibre; 3 g Protein; 244 mg Sodium

Spiced Sweet Pecans

These nut-torious nibblies won't stay in your candy bowl for long! You can also use them for a salad topping.

Granulated sugar	3 tbsp.	50 mL
Butter (or hard margarine), melted	2 tbsp.	30 mL
Balsamic vinegar	1 tbsp.	15 mL
Ground cinnamon	1/2 tsp.	2 mL
Paprika	1/2 tsp.	2 mL
Cayenne pepper	1/4 tsp.	1 mL
Salt	1/4 tsp.	1 mL
Pepper	1/4 tsp.	1 mL
Pecan halves	2 1/2 cups	625 mL

Preheat oven to 350°F (175°C). Combine first 8 ingredients in large bowl.

Add pecans. Stir until coated. Transfer to baking sheet with sides, lined with greased foil. Bake for about 12 minutes until toasted and fragrant. Remove baking sheet to wire rack to cool. Makes about 2 1/2 cups (625 mL).

1/4 cup (60 mL): 239 Calories; 23.4 g Total Fat (12.6 g Mono, 6.4 g Poly, 3.3 g Sat); 6 mg Cholesterol; 8 g Carbohydrate; 3 g Fibre; 3 g Protein; 75 mg Sodium

Go-Withs

Garlic Croutons

These are so delicious and so quick and easy to make, those rock-hard boxed croutons will pale by comparison. Great in salads, soups or casseroles.

Sourdough (or French) bread loaf	1/2	1/2
Butter (or hard margarine)	2 tbsp.	30 mL
Olive (or cooking) oil	2 tbsp.	30 mL
Garlic cloves, minced	3	3
(or 3/4 tsp., 4 mL, powder)		
Parsley flakes	1/2 tsp.	2 mL
Salt, sprinkle		
Pepper, sprinkle		

Preheat oven to 325°F (160°C). Remove crust from bread. Cut bread into 1/2 inch (12 mm) slices. Stacking 2 or 3 slices together, cut into 1/2 inch (12 mm) cubes. Transfer bread cubes to extra-large bowl.

Heat and stir next 4 ingredients in large frying pan on medium until butter is melted. Drizzle half of butter mixture over bread cubes. Toss. Drizzle with remaining butter mixture. Toss until coated. Spread evenly on ungreased baking sheet with sides.

Sprinkle with salt and pepper. Bake for about 20 minutes until crisp and golden. Remove baking sheet to wire rack to cool. Makes about 4 cups (1 L).

1/4 cup (60 mL): 31 Calories; 3.1 g Total Fat (1.6 g Mono, 0.2 g Poly, 1.1 g Sat); 4 mg Cholesterol; 1 g Carbohydrate; trace Fibre; trace Protein; 18 mg Sodium

Variation: Sprinkle with various dried herbs for herb-seasoned croutons.

Go-Withs

Speedy Sassy Salsa

This fresh pepper-packed salsa is sassy, indeed! The heat lingers and won't disappoint. If you can, make this salsa a day in advance to let the flavours really develop—but it's still delicious when it's brand spankin' fresh. Serve with tortilla chips or grilled meats. Store in an airtight container in the fridge for up to four days.

Small green peppers, coarsely chopped	2	2
Small onion, cut into 4 pieces	1	1
Coarsely chopped fresh cilantro or parsley, lightly packed	1/2 cup	125 mL
Fresh jalapeño peppers (see Coach, page 75), coarsely chopped	2	2
Garlic clove	1	1
Can of diced tomatoes (with juice)	28 oz.	796 mL
Can of tomato paste	5 1/2 oz.	156 mL
Lime juice	3 tbsp.	50 mL
Ground cumin	1 tsp.	5 mL
Hot sauce (optional)	1 tsp.	5 mL

Put first 5 ingredients into blender or food processor. Process with on/off motion until finely chopped. Transfer to large bowl.

Put remaining 5 ingredients into blender or food processor. Process until smooth. Add to vegetable mixture. Stir. Makes about 6 cups (1.5 L).

1/4 cup (60 mL): 18 Calories; 0.1 g Total Fat (trace Mono, trace Poly, trace Sat); 0 mg Cholesterol; 4 g Carbohydrate; 1 g Fibre; 1 g Protein; 102 mg Sodium

Pictured on page 17.

If a recipe calls for less than an entire can of tomato paste, freeze the unopened can for 30 minutes. Open both ends and push the contents through one end. Slice off only what you need. Freeze the remaining paste in a resealable freezer bag or plastic wrap for future use.

Lemon Pepper Muffins

The peppery bursts of flavour in these fresh-tasting lemon muffins make them a perfect companion for fish or seafood soups and salads. If you don't have seasoned salt, table salt can be used in a pinch.

All-purpose flour	2 1/4 cups	550 mL
Baking powder	2 1/2 tsp.	12 mL
Pepper	1 1/2 tsp.	7 mL
Seasoned salt	1/4 tsp.	1 mL
Large eggs, fork-beaten	3	3
Milk	2/3 cup	150 mL
Butter (or hard margarine), melted	1/2 cup	125 mL
Granulated sugar	1/4 cup	60 mL
Lemon juice	3 tbsp.	50 mL
Grated lemon zest (see Coach, below)	2 tsp.	10 mL
Chopped green onion	1/4 cup	60 mL

Preheat oven to 400°F (205°C). Measure first 4 ingredients into medium bowl. Stir. Make a well in centre.

Combine next 6 ingredients in small bowl. Add to well.

Add green onion. Stir until just moistened. Fill 24 greased mini-muffin cups 3/4 full. Bake for about 12 minutes until wooden pick inserted in centre of muffin comes out clean. Let stand in pan for 5 minutes. Remove muffins from pan and place on wire rack to cool. Make 24 mini-muffins.

1 mini-muffin: 93 Calories; 4.5 g Total Fat (1.3 g Mono, 0.2 g Poly, 2.6 g Sat); 34 mg Cholesterol; 11 g Carbohydrate; trace Fibre; 2 g Protein; 80 mg Sodium

Pictured on page 89.

When a recipe calls for grated lemon zest and juice, it's easier to grate the lemon first, then juice it. Be careful not to grate down to the pith (white part of the peel), which is bitter and best avoided.

Lemon Butter Sauce

This little go-with is so unexpected that your guests will surely feel pampered. Serve warm with muffins, pancakes, waffles, ice cream—even grilled chicken!

Granulated sugar	1/2 cup	125 mL
Cornstarch	2 tbsp.	30 mL
Grated lemon zest	1/2 tsp.	2 mL
Water	1 cup	250 mL
Lemon juice	2 tbsp.	30 mL
Butter	2 tbsp.	30 mL

Combine first 3 ingredients in small saucepan.

Add water and lemon juice. Heat and stir until boiling and thickened. Remove from heat.

Add butter. Stir until melted. Makes about 1 1/3 cups (325 mL).

2 tbsp. (30 mL): 60 Calories; 2.1 g Total Fat (0.6 g Mono, 0.1 g Poly, 1.3 g Sat); 6 mg Cholesterol; 11 g Carbohydrate; trace Fibre; trace Protein; 15 mg Sodium

Creamy Horseradish Sauce

Perk up burgers, roast beef or even mashed potatoes with this flavourful sauce. Store in an airtight container in the fridge for up to a week.

Block of cream cheese, softened	8 oz.	250 g
Prepared horseradish	2 tbsp.	30 mL
Lemon juice	1 tbsp.	15 mL
Granulated sugar	1 tsp.	5 mL
Salt	1/4 tsp.	1 mL
Milk	1/3 cup	75 mL
Chopped fresh chives	1 tbsp.	15 mL

Beat first 5 ingredients in medium bowl, scraping down sides if necessary, until smooth.

Slowly add milk, beating constantly, until combined. Add chives. Stir. Makes about 2 cups (500 mL).

2 tbsp. (30 mL): 52 Calories; 4.8 g Total Fat (1.4 g Mono, 0.2 g Poly, 3.0 g Sat); 15 mg Cholesterol; 1 g Carbohydrate; trace Fibre; 1 g Protein; 84 mg Sodium

Go-Withs **81**

Blueberry Maple Topping

Perfect with pancakes or ice cream. Will keep in the fridge for two weeks.

Water	2 tbsp.	30 mL
Cornstarch	2 tsp.	10 mL
Fresh (or frozen) blueberries	1 1/2 cups	375 mL
Granulated sugar	1/4 cup	60 mL
Maple (or maple-flavoured) syrup	1/4 cup	60 mL

Stir water into cornstarch in small cup.

Combine remaining 3 ingredients in small saucepan. Bring to a boil ron medium. Reduce heat to medium-low. Simmer, uncovered, for about 5 minutes, stirring occasionally, until blueberries are soft. Stir cornstarch mixture. Add to blueberry mixture. Heat and stir until boiling and thickened. Makes about 1 1/4 cups (300 mL).

1/4 cup (60 mL): 104 Calories; 0.3 g Total Fat (trace Mono, trace Poly, trace Sat); 0 mg Cholesterol; 26 g Carbohydrate; 1 g Fibre; trace Protein; 2 mg Sodium

Tomato Basil Sauce

Make your own tomato sauce. Great with pasta, chicken or fish.

Olive (or cooking) oil	1 tbsp.	15 mL
Chopped onion	1 cup	250 mL
Dried basil	2 tsp.	10 mL
Garlic cloves, minced	2	2
(or 1/2 tsp., 2 mL, powder)		
Can of diced tomatoes (with juice)	28 oz.	796 mL
Balsamic vinegar	1 tbsp.	15 mL
Granulated sugar	1 tsp.	5 mL
Salt	1/2 tsp.	2 mL
Pepper	1/4 tsp.	1 mL

Heat olive oil in medium saucepan on medium. Add next 3 ingredients. Cook, uncovered, for about 5 minutes, stirring often, until onion is softened.

Add remaining 5 ingredients. Stir. Bring to a boil on medium. Cook for 5 minutes, stirring occasionally, to blend flavours. Carefully process with hand blender or in blender until smooth (see Safety Tip). Makes about 3 1/2 cups (875 mL).

1/2 cup (125 mL): 51 Calories; 2.0 g Total Fat (1.4 g Mono, 0.2 g Poly, 0.3 g Sat); 0 mg Cholesterol; 8 g Carbohydrate; trace Fibre; 1 g Protein; 478 mg Sodium

Safety Tip: Follow blender manufacturer's instructions for processing hot liquids.

Go-Withs

Kickin' Shrimp Sauce

This spicy, sweet and tangy cocktail sauce will knock your socks off.
Serve alongside chilled cooked shrimp or crispy fish fillets. Store in an airtight
container in the refrigerator for up to 10 days—if it lasts that long!

Chili sauce	1/2 cup	125 mL
Creamed horseradish	2 1/2 tbsp.	37 mL
Lemon juice	2 tbsp.	30 mL
Grated lemon zest	1/2 tsp.	2 mL

Combine all 4 ingredients in small bowl. Makes about 3/4 cup (175 mL).

2 tbsp. (30 mL): 10 Calories; 0.1 g Total Fat (trace Mono, trace Poly, trace Sat);
0 mg Cholesterol; 2 g Carbohydrate; 1 g Fibre; trace Protein; 26 mg Sodium

Honey Basil Vinaigrette

Make your everyday mixed greens special by adding this
sweet and savoury homemade dressing.

Olive (or cooking) oil	2/3 cup	150 mL
Apple cider vinegar	3 tbsp.	50 mL
Apple juice	3 tbsp.	50 mL
Chopped fresh basil	2 tbsp.	30 mL
(or 1 1/2 tsp., 7 mL, dried)		
Liquid honey	1 tbsp.	15 mL
Dry mustard	1 tsp.	5 mL
Salt	1/4 tsp.	1 mL

Combine all 7 ingredients in jar with tight-fitting lid. Shake well.
Makes about 1 cup (250 mL).

2 tbsp. (30 mL): 159 Calories; 16.6 g Total Fat (12.2 g Mono, 1.4 g Poly, 2.2 g Sat);
0 mg Cholesterol; 3 g Carbohydrate; trace Fibre; trace Protein; 69 mg Sodium

COACH

If you're a big fan of fresh herbs, try adding a little fresh
basil to your greens for an added layer of freshness.

Basic Beef Sukiyaki

Everyone needs a quick and easy stir-fry in their cooking repertoire.
Get some rice cooking right away so you have something to put your sukiyaki
on. And if you'd rather leave the spinach to the Popeyes of the world,
use half a head of Chinese cabbage, cut into short pieces, instead.

Prepared beef broth	1/3 cup	75 mL
Brown sugar, packed	1/4 cup	60 mL
Soy sauce	3 tbsp.	50 mL
Cornstarch	1 1/2 tsp.	7 mL
Cooking oil	2 tsp.	10 mL
Beef top sirloin steak, cut into thin, short strips	1 lb.	454 g
Box of frozen chopped spinach, thawed and squeezed dry	10 oz.	300 g
Sliced fresh white mushrooms	1 cup	250 mL
Green onions, chopped	4	4

Heat large frying pan or wok on medium-high until very hot. Meanwhile, combine first 4 ingredients in small bowl. Set aside.

Add cooking oil to frying pan. Add beef. Stir-fry for 2 to 4 minutes until desired doneness.

Add remaining 3 ingredients. Stir-fry for about 2 minutes until liquid is evaporated. Stir cornstarch mixture. Add to beef mixture. Stir well. Reduce heat to medium. Heat and stir for about 1 minute until boiling and thickened. Makes about 4 cups (1 L).

1 cup (250 mL): 296 Calories; 10.7 g Total Fat (4.6 g Mono, 1.0 g Poly, 3.3 g Sat); 60 mg Cholesterol; 22 g Carbohydrate; 2 g Fibre; 29 g Protein; 822 mg Sodium

TOFU SUKIYAKI: Use same amount of cubed firm tofu instead of beef.

Feel Good Cheeseburger Macaroni

Had a hard day? This is the ultimate comfort food.
And if you want to spice things up a bit, use cans of seasoned
tomatoes—there are quite a few varieties out there.

Water	8 cups	2 L
Salt	1 tsp.	5 mL
Elbow macaroni	2 cups	500 mL
Cooking oil	1 tsp.	5 mL
Lean ground beef	1 lb.	454 g
Chopped onion	1 cup	250 mL
Garlic clove, minced	1	1
(or 1/4 tsp., 1 mL, powder)		
Cans of stewed tomatoes	2	2
(14 oz., 398 mL, each), coarsely chopped		
Ketchup	1/4 cup	60 mL
Italian seasoning	1/2 tsp.	2 mL
Salt	1/2 tsp.	2 mL
Pepper	1/2 tsp.	2 mL
Grated sharp Cheddar cheese	1 cup	250 mL
Grated sharp Cheddar cheese	1/2 cup	125 mL

Combine water and salt in large saucepan. Bring to a boil. Add macaroni.
Boil, uncovered, for 6 to 8 minutes, stirring occasionally, until tender
but firm. Drain. Cover to keep warm.

Meanwhile, heat cooking oil in large frying pan on medium-high.
Add next 3 ingredients. Scramble-fry for 8 to 10 minutes until beef
is browned. Drain.

Add next 5 ingredients. Stir. Bring to a boil. Reduce heat to medium.
Cook for 5 minutes to blend flavours.

Add first amount of cheese and macaroni. Cook and stir for about
2 minutes until heated through. Remove from heat.

Sprinkle with second amount of cheese. Makes about 8 1/2 cups (2.1 L).

1 cup (250 mL): 335 Calories; 13.0 g Total Fat (4.6 g Mono, 0.7 g Poly, 6.6 g Sat);
63 mg Cholesterol; 28 g Carbohydrate; 1 g Fibre; 26 g Protein; 623 mg Sodium

Variation: Use Mexican or Italian cheese blend instead of Cheddar.

Mains — Beef

Pineapple Meatballs

Meatballs can be very chic when they're flavoured with ginger and soy sauce, and are served over a bed of rice. Just get your rice cooking while you make the meatballs.

Large egg, fork-beaten	1	1
Fine dry bread crumbs	3/4 cup	175 mL
Milk	1/4 cup	60 mL
Soy sauce	1 tbsp.	15 mL
Finely grated gingerroot	2 tsp.	10 mL
(or 1/2 tsp., 2 mL, ground ginger)		
Garlic cloves, minced	2	2
(or 1/2 tsp., 2 mL, powder)		
Lean ground beef	1 lb.	454 g
Cooking oil	1 tsp.	5 mL
Chopped green pepper	1/2 cup	125 mL
Can of pineapple tidbits (with juice)	14 oz.	398 mL
Brown sugar, packed	1/3 cup	75 mL
Rice vinegar	1/4 cup	60 mL
Hoisin sauce	2 tbsp.	30 mL
Water	2 tbsp.	30 mL
Cornstarch	1 tbsp.	15 mL

Preheat oven to 400°F (205°C). Combine first 6 ingredients in large bowl.

Add beef. Mix well. Roll into 1 1/2 inch (3.8 cm) balls. Arrange on greased baking sheet with sides. Bake for 15 minutes. Makes about 24 meatballs.

Meanwhile, heat cooking oil in large frying pan on medium-high. Add green pepper. Cook for 2 to 4 minutes, stirring occasionally, until tender-crisp.

Combine next 4 ingredients in small bowl. Add to green pepper. Add meatballs. Stir. Reduce heat to medium-low. Simmer, covered, for about 3 minutes until meatballs are fully cooked and internal temperature reaches 160°F (71°C).

Stir water into cornstarch in small cup. Add to meatball mixture. Heat and stir for about 2 minutes until boiling and thickened. Makes about 5 cups (1.25 L).

(continued on next page)

Mains — Beef

1 cup (250 mL): 402 Calories; 15.6 g Total Fat (7.0 g Mono, 1.0 g Poly, 5.7 g Sat); 92 mg Cholesterol; 42 g Carbohydrate; 2 g Fibre; 22 g Protein; 490 mg Sodium

Meat thermometers are great investments for any cook, but especially rookie cooks. With their clearly labelled temperatures, they let you know, for sure, that your meat is properly cooked.

Your Best Barbecued Steak

Nothing wins rave reviews from both the ladies and the men like a fantastic barbecued steak.

Cooking oil	2 tsp.	10 mL
Dijon mustard	2 tsp.	10 mL
No-Salt Barbecue Spice, page 76	1 1/2 tsp.	7 mL
Beef rib-eye steak	1 lb.	454 g

Preheat gas barbecue to medium-high. Combine first 3 ingredients in small cup.

Rub both sides of steak with mustard mixture. Cook on greased grill for 4 to 5 minutes per side until desired doneness. Transfer to plate. Cover with foil. Let stand for 5 minutes. Cut into 4 equal portions. Serves 4.

1 serving: 241 Calories; 15.9 g Total Fat (6.9 g Mono, 1.2 g Poly, 5.5 g Sat); 102 mg Cholesterol; 1 g Carbohydrate; trace Fibre; 22 g Protein; 79 mg Sodium

Pictured on page 90.

To assess doneness of a steak, follow these guidelines:
rare: seared with a 75 per cent red inside
medium rare: seared with a 50 per cent red inside
medium: seared with a 25 per cent pink inside
medium well: cooked throughout with a hint of pink in the middle
well done: no hint of pink on the inside

Mega Meatball Sandwiches

*You can spice up this cheesy bad boy by adding 1/4 to 1/2 tsp.
(1 to 2 mL) dried crushed chilies to the sauce.*

Cooking oil	1 tsp.	5 mL
Chopped onion	1/2 cup	125 mL
Can of tomato sauce	14 oz.	398 mL
Bay leaves	2	2
Italian seasoning	1 1/2 tsp.	7 mL
Pepper	1/4 tsp.	1 mL
Frozen cooked meatballs	32	32
Baguette bread loaf	1	1
Grated Mexican cheese blend	1 cup	250 mL

Heat cooking oil in large frying pan on medium. Add onion. Cook for about 5 minutes, stirring often, until onion starts to soften.

Add next 4 ingredients. Stir.

Add meatballs. Stir. Simmer, covered, for about 8 minutes, stirring occasionally, until heated through. Discard bay leaves.

Preheat broiler. Cut baguette crosswise into 4 equal portions. Cut portions horizontally lengthwise almost, but not quite through, to other side. Place, cut-side up, on ungreased baking sheet with sides. Spoon meatball mixture over top. Sprinkle with cheese. Broil on top rack in oven for 2 to 4 minutes until cheese is melted. Makes 4 sandwiches.

1 sandwich: 674 Calories; 39.2 g Total Fat (13.3 g Mono, 1.8 g Poly, 16.4 g Sat); 211 mg Cholesterol; 32 g Carbohydrate; 3 g Fibre; 46 g Protein; 1183 mg Sodium

Pictured on page 17.

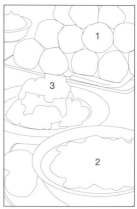

1. Lemon Pepper Muffins, page 80
2. Thoroughly Modern Chili, page 116
3. Berry Cake Cups, page 136

Props courtesy of: Pier 1 Imports
Winners Stores

Tater Surprise

When we say trouble-free, we mean trouble-free—
you can even serve this one straight out of the frying pan!

Frozen potato tots (gems or puffs)	40	40
Cooking oil	1 tsp.	5 mL
Lean ground beef	1 lb.	454 g
Chopped onion	1/4 cup	60 mL
Frozen mixed peas and carrots	2 cups	500 mL
Can of condensed cream of mushroom soup	10 oz.	284 mL
Barbecue sauce	2 tbsp.	30 mL

Preheat oven to 450°F (230°C). Arrange potato tots in single layer on ungreased baking sheet with sides. Bake for about 15 minutes until golden.

Meanwhile, heat cooking oil in large frying pan on medium-high. Add beef and onion. Scramble-fry for 8 to 10 minutes until beef is browned. Drain.

Add remaining 3 ingredients. Stir. Arrange potato tots in single layer over beef mixture. Reduce heat to medium. Cook for 2 to 3 minutes until bubbling and vegetables are tender. Serves 4.

1 serving: 536 Calories; 24.0 g Total Fat (8.5 g Mono, 0.9 g Poly, 6.9 g Sat); 92 mg Cholesterol; 39 g Carbohydrate; 6 g Fibre; 40 g Protein; 1162 mg Sodium

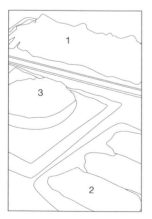

1. Thai-rrific Basil Stir-Fry, page 93
2. Your Best Barbecued Steak, page 87
3. Cheesy Portobellos, page 92

Props courtesy of: Pier 1 Imports
Winners Stores

Cheesy Portobellos

Now this is the kind of entree you'd expect to see in a very popular,
big-city bistro. With its smoky bacon flavour, feta and Brie cheese,
no one's going to believe it was made by a rookie.

Portobello mushrooms (about 4 inch, 10 cm, diameter), stems removed	4	4
Salt	1/4 tsp.	1 mL
Pepper	1/4 tsp.	1 mL
Lean ground beef	1/2 lb.	225 g
Chopped onion	1/2 cup	125 mL
Bacon slices, chopped	4	4
Garlic clove, minced (or 1/4 tsp., 1 mL, powder)	1	1
Brie cheese round, chopped	4 oz.	125 g
Crumbled feta cheese	1/2 cup	125 mL
Chopped fresh basil	2 tbsp.	30 mL
Finely chopped chipotle pepper in adobo sauce (see Coach, page 133)	1/2 tsp.	2 mL

Preheat oven to 400°F (205°C). Using small spoon, remove and discard gills from mushroom caps. Sprinkle with salt and pepper. Place in greased 9 x 13 inch (22 x 33 cm) pan. Bake for about 8 minutes until starting to soften.

Meanwhile, heat large frying pan on medium-high. Add next 4 ingredients. Scramble-fry for 8 to 10 minutes until bacon is almost crisp and beef is browned. Drain.

Add remaining 4 ingredients. Stir. Preheat broiler. Spoon beef mixture into mushrooms. Broil on centre rack in oven for about 5 minutes until filling is bubbling and golden. Makes 4 stuffed mushrooms.

1 stuffed mushroom: 349 Calories; 21.2 g Total Fat (7.1 g Mono, 0.9 g Poly, 11.6 g Sat); 99 mg Cholesterol; 8 g Carbohydrate; 2 g Fibre; 31 g Protein; 742 mg Sodium

Pictured on page 90.

Thai-rrific Basil Stir-Fry

Have someone you want to impress? Here's a hint: because
Thai flavours taste exotic, people automatically think Thai dishes
are hard to make. Serve this one over rice.

Prepared beef broth	1/4 cup	60 mL
Lime juice	2 tbsp.	30 mL
Brown sugar, packed	2 tbsp.	30 mL
Soy sauce	1 tbsp.	15 mL
Cornstarch	2 tsp.	10 mL
Cooking oil	1 tbsp.	15 mL
Beef top sirloin steak, cut into thin, short strips	1 lb.	454 g
Garlic clove, minced (or 1/4 tsp., 1 mL, powder)	1	1
Dried crushed chilies	1 tsp.	5 mL
Sliced onion	1 cup	250 mL
Sliced red pepper	1 cup	250 mL
Chopped fresh basil	1/4 cup	60 mL
Chopped dry-roasted peanuts (optional)	1/4 cup	60 mL

Heat large frying pan or wok on medium-high until very hot.
Meanwhile, combine first 5 ingredients in small cup. Set aside.

Add cooking oil to frying pan. Add next 3 ingredients. Stir-fry for about
2 to 4 minutes until beef reaches desired doneness. Transfer to plate.
Cover to keep warm.

Add onion and red pepper to same frying pan. Stir-fry for about 2 minutes
until tender-crisp. Add beef mixture. Stir cornstarch mixture. Add to beef
mixture. Heat and stir for about 1 minute until boiling and thickened.

Add basil. Stir. Sprinkle peanuts over top. Makes about 2 1/2 cups
(625 mL). Serves 4.

1 serving: 217 Calories; 7.1 g Total Fat (3.1 g Mono, trace Poly, 2.8 g Sat); 60 mg Cholesterol;
14 g Carbohydrate; 1 g Fibre; 23 g Protein; 325 mg Sodium

Pictured on page 90.

Lazy Lasagna

*This lasagna isn't lacking motivation—you're the one who gets
to be lazy! It isn't baked or layered—but the taste is all lasagna!
Double the amount of chilies if you like a little heat.*

Water	8 cups	2 L
Salt	1 tsp.	5 mL
Lasagna noodles, broken into 4 pieces each	8	8
Cooking oil	1 tbsp.	15 mL
Sliced fresh white mushrooms	2 cups	500 mL
Chopped green pepper	1 cup	250 mL
Chopped onion	1 cup	250 mL
Dried crushed chilies	1/2 tsp.	2 mL
Tomato pasta sauce	2 cups	500 mL
Can of diced tomatoes (with juice)	14 oz.	398 mL
Frozen cooked meatballs	20	20
Dried oregano	1 tsp.	5 mL
Dried basil	1/2 tsp.	2 mL
Pepper	1/4 tsp.	1 mL
Grated mozzarella cheese	2 cups	500 mL

Combine water and salt in large saucepan or Dutch oven. Bring to a boil.
Add noodles. Boil, uncovered, for about 10 minutes, stirring occasionally,
until tender but firm. Drain. Return to same pot. Cover to keep warm.

Meanwhile, heat cooking oil in large frying pan on medium-high. Add next
4 ingredients. Cook for about 5 minutes, stirring occasionally, until onion
is softened.

Add next 6 ingredients. Stir. Bring to a boil. Reduce heat to medium. Cook,
covered, for about 5 minutes until heated through. Add noodles. Stir.

Preheat broiler. Sprinkle cheese over noodle mixture. Broil on centre rack in
oven (see Coach, page 95) for about 5 minutes until cheese is melted and
golden. Serves 4.

*1 serving: 810 Calories; 35.4 g Total Fat (13.8 g Mono, 2.5 g Poly, 14.7 g Sat); 162 mg Cholesterol;
75 g Carbohydrate; 6 g Fibre; 48 g Protein; 1378 mg Sodium*

Stroganoff Noodles

Named after Russian nobility, beef Stroganoff is a rich and decadent delight.
Add some steamed veggies and dinner is served. (Save the leftover onion soup
mix for other recipes. Or you can rub it on a roast before cooking
for a quick and easy seasoning.)

Water	12 cups	3 L
Salt	1 1/2 tsp.	7 mL
Medium egg noodles	7 cups	1.75 L
Cooking oil	1 tsp.	5 mL
Lean ground beef	1 lb.	454 g
Can of condensed cream of mushroom soup	10 oz.	284 mL
Milk	1 cup	250 mL
Dry onion soup mix (stir before measuring)	2 tbsp.	30 mL
Sour cream	1/2 cup	125 mL

Chopped fresh dill, for garnish

Combine water and salt in Dutch oven. Bring to a boil. Add noodles.
Boil, uncovered, for 5 to 6 minutes, stirring occasionally, until tender
but firm. Drain. Return to same pot. Cover to keep warm.

Meanwhile, heat cooking oil in large frying pan on medium-high.
Add beef. Scramble-fry for 8 to 10 minutes until browned. Drain.
Reduce heat to medium.

Stir next 3 ingredients in small bowl until smooth. Add to beef.
Cook for about 5 minutes, stirring occasionally, until boiling
and thickened.

Add sour cream and noodles. Stir well.

Garnish with dill. Makes about 10 cups (2.5 L).

1 cup (250 mL): 775 Calories; 15.5 g Total Fat (3.2 g Mono, 2.4 g Poly, 5.6 g Sat);
208 mg Cholesterol; 119 g Carbohydrate; 5 g Fibre; 39 g Protein; 562 mg Sodium

COACH

When baking or broiling food in a frying pan with a handle
that isn't ovenproof, wrap the handle in tinfoil and keep it
to the front of the oven, away from the element.

Crispy Chicken Cutlets

These crisp, juicy golden brown cutlets are packed with flavour. Don't be afraid to try this versatile coating on pork or turkey cutlets, as well.

All-purpose flour	1/3 cup	75 mL
Large eggs, fork-beaten	2	2
Milk	2 tbsp.	30 mL
Fine dry bread crumbs	3/4 cup	175 mL
Paprika	2 tsp.	10 mL
Salt	1 tsp.	5 mL
Pepper	1 tsp.	5 mL
Garlic powder	1/2 tsp.	2 mL
Ground cinnamon	1/4 tsp.	1 mL
Cooking oil	2 tbsp.	30 mL
Chicken breast cutlets (about 1 lb., 454 g)	4	4
Chopped fresh parsley	2 tbsp.	30 mL

Measure flour onto large plate.

Beat eggs and milk with fork in large shallow dish.

Combine next 6 ingredients in small cup. Transfer to separate large plate.

Heat cooking oil in large frying pan on medium. Press both sides of chicken into flour. Dip into egg mixture. Press both sides of chicken into crumb mixture until coated. Discard any remaining flour, egg mixture and bread crumb mixture. Arrange chicken in frying pan. Cook for about 5 minutes per side until golden and no longer pink inside.

Sprinkle with parsley. Makes 4 cutlets.

1 cutlet: 392 Calories; 15.0 g Total Fat (7.2 g Mono, 3.8 g Poly, 2.8 g Sat); 173 mg Cholesterol; 19 g Carbohydrate; 1 g Fibre; 43 g Protein; 686 mg Sodium

South Seas Chicken

Ahoy, matey! There'll be no mutiny when your guests taste this sweet-and-spicy bounty. Serve on rice, couscous or chickpeas.

Pineapple juice	1 cup	250 mL
Apple cider vinegar	2 tbsp.	30 mL
Lime juice	2 tbsp.	30 mL
Brown sugar, packed	1 tbsp.	15 mL
Cornstarch	2 tsp.	10 mL
Garlic powder	1 tsp.	5 mL
Ground cinnamon	1 tsp.	5 mL
Ground ginger	1 tsp.	5 mL
Ground allspice	1/2 tsp.	2 mL
Cayenne pepper	1/8 tsp.	0.5 mL
Cooking oil	2 tsp.	10 mL
Boneless, skinless chicken thighs, cut into bite-sized pieces	1 lb.	454 g

Chopped fresh parsley, for garnish

Combine first 10 ingredients in small bowl.

Heat large frying pan on medium-high until very hot. Add cooking oil. Add chicken. Stir-fry for about 5 minutes until chicken is no longer pink inside. Reduce heat to medium-low. Add pineapple juice mixture. Heat and stir until boiling and thickened.

Garnish with parsley. Makes about 2 1/2 cups (625 mL).

1 cup (250 mL): 390 Calories; 16.1 g Total Fat (6.7 g Mono, 4.0 g Poly, 3.6 g Sat); 122 mg Cholesterol; 26 g Carbohydrate; 1 g Fibre; 34 g Protein; 120 mg Sodium

COACH

Wondering if you have to be specific with the cut of chicken when you're making dishes like these? No! You can easily substitute other cuts, as long as you keep the boneless weight the same.

Easy Quesadillas

Want to add an extra dimension to these fresh and flavourful quesadillas
(pronounced keh-sah-DEE-yahs)? Try using any of the different flavoured
tortillas available at your supermarket. Serve with salsa and sour cream,
and add a big green salad for a complete meal.

Cooking oil	1 tsp.	5 mL
Sliced fresh white mushrooms	2 cups	500 mL
Chopped green pepper	2/3 cup	150 mL
Chopped onion	1/3 cup	75 mL
Chopped cooked chicken (see Coach, page 31)	1 1/2 cups	375 mL
Basil pesto	1/4 cup	60 mL
Flour tortillas (9 inch, 22 cm, diameter)	4	4
Grated mozzarella cheese	1 1/3 cups	325 mL
Crumbled feta cheese	3/4 cup	175 mL
Cooking spray		

Preheat oven to 425°F (220°C). Heat cooking oil in large frying pan on medium. Add next 3 ingredients. Cook for 8 to 10 minutes, stirring often, until onion is softened and liquid is evaporated.

Add chicken and pesto. Stir.

Spoon chicken mixture evenly over half of each tortilla.

Sprinkle mozzarella and feta cheese over chicken mixture. Fold tortillas in half to cover filling. Press down lightly. Arrange tortillas on greased baking sheet with sides.

Spray tortillas with cooking spray. Bake for about 10 minutes until crisp and starting to brown. Cut tortillas in half. Makes 8 wedges.

1 wedge: 296 Calories; 17.5 g Total Fat (5.1 g Mono, 2.8 g Poly, 7.0 g Sat); 68 mg Cholesterol; 13 g Carbohydrate; 1 g Fibre; 21 g Protein; 478 mg Sodium

First-Class Chicken Curry

Mango and peaches add a gentle sweetness to this delicious chicken curry served over a bed of rice. Start the rice cooking before you start preparing the curry.

Water	3 cups	750 mL
Salt	1/2 tsp.	2 mL
Long grain white rice	1 1/2 cups	375 mL
Cooking oil	1 tbsp.	15 mL
Lean ground chicken	1 lb.	454 g
Chopped onion	1/2 cup	125 mL
Coleslaw mix	2 cups	500 mL
Mango chutney, larger pieces chopped	1/2 cup	125 mL
Prepared chicken broth	1/2 cup	125 mL
Curry powder	1 tsp.	5 mL
Finely grated gingerroot	1 tsp.	5 mL
(or 1/4 tsp., 1 mL, ground ginger)		
Garlic powder	1/4 tsp.	1 mL
Ground cumin	1/4 tsp.	1 mL
Can of sliced peaches in juice,	14 oz.	398 mL
drained and chopped		
Plain yogurt	1/2 cup	125 mL

Combine water and salt in medium saucepan. Bring to a boil. Add rice. Stir. Reduce heat to medium-low. Simmer, covered, for about 20 minutes, without stirring, until liquid is absorbed. Remove from heat. Let stand, covered, for 5 minutes. Fluff with fork.

Meanwhile, heat cooking oil in large frying pan on medium-high. Add chicken and onion. Scramble-fry for 8 to 10 minutes until chicken is no longer pink.

Add next 7 ingredients. Stir. Cook for about 5 minutes, stirring occasionally, until coleslaw is tender-crisp.

Add peaches. Cook and stir for about 1 minute until heated through. Remove from heat. Add yogurt. Stir. Serve over rice. Serves 4.

1 serving: 732 Calories; 22.9 g Total Fat (2.3 g Mono, 1.3 g Poly, 0.5 g Sat); 1 mg Cholesterol; 103 g Carbohydrate; 5 g Fibre; 29 g Protein; 915 mg Sodium

Chicken Tofu Stir-Fry

This sweet-and-sour, spicy stir-fry comes together in a snap.
Using ground chicken in stir-fries cuts down the prep time, and tofu is a great
addition to spicy dishes because it takes on the flavour of the ingredients
it is cooked with—and it counts as extra protein.

Cooking oil	2 tsp.	10 mL
Chopped onion	1 cup	250 mL
Lean ground chicken	1/2 lb.	225 g
Garlic cloves, minced	2	2
(or 1/2 tsp., 2 mL, powder)		
Chopped red pepper	1 cup	250 mL
Chopped yellow pepper	1 cup	250 mL
Soy sauce	3 tbsp.	50 mL
Brown sugar, packed	2 tbsp.	30 mL
Lime juice	2 tbsp.	30 mL
Sweet chili sauce	2 tbsp.	30 mL
Pepper	1/4 tsp.	1 mL
Diced firm tofu	2 cups	500 mL

Heat cooking oil in large frying pan on medium-high. Add next 3 ingredients. Scramble-fry for 3 to 5 minutes until chicken is no longer pink.

Add next 7 ingredients. Stir. Cook, covered, for 2 to 4 minutes until peppers are tender-crisp.

Add tofu. Heat and stir for about 1 minute until heated through. Makes about 4 1/2 cups (1.1 L).

1 cup (250 mL): 239 Calories; 11.0 g Total Fat (1.6 g Mono, 1.8 g Poly, 0.5 g Sat);
0 mg Cholesterol; 18 g Carbohydrate; 2 g Fibre; 18 g Protein; 629 mg Sodium

Chicken Mole

No need to go underground in search of an earthy chicken stew! Mole (pronounced MOH-lay) is a traditional spicy Mexican sauce that contains just enough cocoa to make it unique. You'll save time by preparing the ingredients for the sauce while the chicken cooks.

Cooking oil	1 tbsp.	15 mL
Boneless, skinless chicken thighs, cut into 1 inch (2.5 cm) pieces	1 lb.	454 g
Chopped onion	1 cup	250 mL
Salt	1/4 tsp.	1 mL
Cayenne pepper	1/4 tsp.	1 mL
Can of tomato sauce	7 1/2 oz.	213 mL
Barbecue sauce	1/2 cup	125 mL
Water	1/4 cup	60 mL
Brown sugar, packed	2 tbsp.	30 mL
Cocoa, sifted if lumpy	2 tbsp.	30 mL
Dark raisins	2 tbsp.	30 mL
Peanut butter	2 tbsp.	30 mL
Chili powder	1 tsp.	5 mL
Garlic powder	1/4 tsp.	1 mL
Ground cinnamon	1/4 tsp.	1 mL

Heat cooking oil in large frying pan on medium-high. Add next 4 ingredients. Cook for about 5 minutes, stirring occasionally, until chicken is no longer pink inside.

Add remaining 10 ingredients. Stir. Reduce heat to medium-low. Cook, covered, for about 10 minutes, stirring occasionally, until chicken is tender. Makes about 3 1/2 cups (875 mL).

1 cup (250 mL): 398 Calories; 18.8 g Total Fat (8.3 g Mono, 4.9 g Poly, 4.0 g Sat); 87 mg Cholesterol; 31 g Carbohydrate; 6 g Fibre; 29 g Protein; 936 mg Sodium

Chicken Picadillo

A Spanish favourite, picadillo (pronounced pee-kah-DEE-yoh) makes great use of common kitchen spices. This recipe may look long but it comes together quite quickly.

Boneless, skinless chicken breast halves	1 lb.	454 g
Salt	1/4 tsp.	1 mL
Pepper	1/8 tsp.	0.5 mL
Ground cumin	1 tsp.	5 mL
Dried basil	1/2 tsp.	2 mL
Dried oregano	1/2 tsp.	2 mL
Garlic powder	1/4 tsp.	1 mL
Ground cinnamon	1/4 tsp.	1 mL
Salt	1/4 tsp.	1 mL
Olive (or cooking) oil	2 tbsp.	30 mL
Chopped onion	1/4 cup	60 mL
Tomato paste (see Coach, page 79)	1 tbsp.	15 mL
Dry (or alcohol-free) red wine	1/4 cup	60 mL
Can of diced tomatoes (with juice)	14 oz.	398 mL
Sliced green olives	1/2 cup	125 mL
Brown sugar, packed	1 tbsp.	15 mL

Cut chicken crosswise into 3/4 inch (2 cm) strips. Sprinkle with salt and pepper.

Combine next 6 ingredients in small cup. Set aside.

Heat olive oil in large frying pan on medium-high. Cook chicken in 2 batches, for about 2 minutes per batch, stirring occasionally, until starting to brown. Transfer to plate. Cover to keep warm.

Add onion to same frying pan. Cook for about 5 minutes, stirring often, until softened.

Add tomato paste and spice mixture. Heat and stir for about 1 minute until fragrant. Add wine. Heat and stir for about 1 minute, scraping any brown bits from bottom of pan, until mixture resembles paste.

(continued on next page)

Add remaining 3 ingredients and chicken. Stir. Reduce heat to medium-low. Cook, covered, for about 5 minutes until chicken is no longer pink inside. Makes about 4 cups (1 L).

1 cup (250 mL): 360 Calories; 15.4 g Total Fat (9.3 g Mono, 2.0 g Poly, 2.8 g Sat); 103 mg Cholesterol; 11 g Carbohydrate; 2 g Fibre; 40 g Protein; 1217 mg Sodium

Pictured on page 54.

COACH

Slicing the chicken breast at a 45° angle will allow it to cook quickly but still remain tender.

Chi-Chi Chicken Fingers

This kiddie-favourite gets glammed up with a hint of lime.

Boneless, skinless chicken breast halves	1 lb.	454 g
Cornflake crumbs	1 cup	250 mL
Grated lime zest	1 tbsp.	15 mL
Granulated sugar	1 tsp.	5 mL
Salt	1 1/2 tsp.	7 mL
Pepper	1/2 tsp.	2 mL
Lime juice	1/4 cup	60 mL
Cooking spray		

Preheat oven to 425°F (220°C). Cut each chicken breast lengthwise into 4 or 5 strips.

Combine next 5 ingredients in small bowl. Transfer to plate.

Measure lime juice into small shallow bowl. Dip chicken into lime juice. Roll in crumb mixture until coated. Arrange on greased baking sheet with sides. Spray chicken with cooking spray. Bake for about 15 minutes until no longer pink inside. Serves 4.

1 serving: 170 Calories; 3.5 g Total Fat (1.3 g Mono, 0.8 g Poly, 0.9 g Sat); 66 mg Cholesterol; 9 g Carbohydrate; trace Fibre; 25 g Protein; 980 mg Sodium

Easy Chicken Paprikash

Prepare an easy bash with this delightful paprikash! This creamy, tomato-laden stew makes quite an elegant entree when served over buttered egg noodles.

All-purpose flour	1/4 cup	60 mL
Paprika	1 tbsp.	15 mL
Salt	1 tsp.	5 mL
Boneless, skinless chicken breast halves, cut into 1 inch (2.5 cm) pieces	1 lb.	454 g
Cooking oil	1 tbsp.	15 mL
Cooking oil	2 tsp.	10 mL
Chopped green pepper	1 cup	250 mL
Chopped onion	1 cup	250 mL
Can of diced tomatoes (with juice)	14 oz.	398 mL
Prepared chicken broth	1/2 cup	125 mL
Apple juice	2 tbsp.	30 mL
Dried dillweed	2 tsp.	10 mL
Sour cream	1/3 cup	75 mL

Combine first 3 ingredients in medium resealable freezer bag. Add chicken. Seal bag. Toss until coated.

Heat first amount of cooking oil in large frying pan on medium-high. Add chicken. Set aside any remaining flour mixture. Cook for about 5 minutes, turning at halftime, until browned. Transfer to plate. Cover to keep warm.

Add second amount of cooking oil to same frying pan. Reduce heat to medium. Add green pepper and onion. Cook for 2 to 4 minutes, stirring often, until vegetables are tender-crisp. Add chicken and reserved flour mixture. Stir.

Add next 4 ingredients. Stir. Bring to a boil. Reduce heat to medium-low. Simmer, covered, for about 5 minutes, stirring occasionally, until vegetables are softened and chicken is no longer pink inside.

Add sour cream. Stir. Makes about 5 cups (1.25 L).

1 cup (250 mL): 239 Calories; 10.3 g Total Fat (4.5 g Mono, 2.2 g Poly, 2.9 g Sat); 59 mg Cholesterol; 15 g Carbohydrate; 1 g Fibre; 22 g Protein; 820 mg Sodium

Pictured on page 107.

Cajun Chicken Po' Boys

Give your mouth a workout with these jaw-extending sandwiches filled with spicy chicken, creamy mayo and crisp lettuce. If you don't have a loaf of French bread, just use kaiser rolls instead.

Cooking oil	2 tsp.	10 mL
Chicken breast cutlets (about 1 lb., 454 g)	4	4
Cajun seasoning	2 tsp.	10 mL
Mayonnaise	1/3 cup	75 mL
Honey Dijon mustard	1 tbsp.	15 mL
French bread loaf, halved horizontally	1	1
Medium tomato, thinly sliced	1	1
Shredded iceberg lettuce, lightly packed	2 cups	500 mL

Heat cooking oil in large frying pan on medium-high. Add chicken. Sprinkle with seasoning. Cook for 3 to 4 minutes per side until no longer pink inside.

Meanwhile, combine mayonnaise and mustard in small cup. Spread evenly on cut sides of bread.

Arrange tomato over mayonnaise mixture on bottom half of loaf. Arrange chicken over tomato.

Top with lettuce. Place top half of loaf, mayonnaise-side down, over lettuce. Cut loaf into 4 equal portions (see Coach, below). Makes 4 sandwiches.

1 sandwich: 514 Calories; 34.2 g Total Fat (15.2 g Mono, 8.6 g Poly, 6.5 g Sat); 110 mg Cholesterol; 24 g Carbohydrate; 2 g Fibre; 26 g Protein; 1154 mg Sodium

Pictured on page 107.

COACH To keep your Po' Boy (and any other big sandwich, for that matter) from falling apart when you cut it, put four toothpicks, spaced evenly apart, into the top half of the loaf to prevent the chicken and bread from shifting.

Chic Chicken Chili

This home-on-the-range special is made chic with the addition of a subtle citrus flavour. This tastes just as good with ground turkey, and you can up the heat factor by adding a can of diced green chilies (4 oz., 113 g).

Cooking oil	1 tsp.	5 mL
Lean ground chicken	1 lb.	454 g
Chopped onion	1 cup	250 mL
Garlic clove, minced	1	1
(or 1/4 tsp., 1 mL, powder)		
Can of diced tomatoes (with juice)	28 oz.	796 mL
Can of black beans, rinsed and drained	19 oz.	540 mL
Can of sliced jalapeño peppers, drained	4 oz.	114 mL
(see Coach, page 75)		
Orange juice	1/4 cup	60 mL
Brown sugar, packed	1 tbsp.	15 mL
Chili powder	1 tsp.	5 mL
Grated orange zest	1 tsp.	5 mL

Heat cooking oil in large frying pan on medium-high. Add next 3 ingredients. Scramble-fry for 8 to 10 minutes until chicken is no longer pink and onion is softened.

Add remaining 7 ingredients. Bring to a boil. Reduce heat to medium-low. Simmer, covered, for 10 minutes to blend flavours. Makes about 6 1/2 cups (1.6 L).

1 cup (250 mL): 238 Calories; 10.4 g Total Fat (0.4 g Mono, 0.3 g Poly, 0.1 g Sat); 0 mg Cholesterol; 23 g Carbohydrate; 5 g Fibre; 17 g Protein; 1013 mg Sodium

Pictured on page 107.

1. Cajun Chicken Po' Boys, page 105
2. Chic Chicken Chili, above
3. Easy Chicken Paprikash, page 104

Props courtesy of: Pier 1 Imports

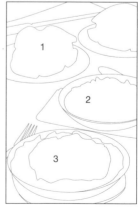

Honey Garlic Salmon

Glazing is a great method of flavouring all sorts of meats with a sweet coating. The simple flavours of honey and garlic go well with salmon.

Brown sugar, packed	2 tbsp.	30 mL
Liquid honey	2 tbsp.	30 mL
Soy sauce	1 tbsp.	15 mL
Cornstarch	2 tsp.	10 mL
Garlic cloves, minced	2	2
(or 1/2 tsp., 2 mL, powder)		
Finely grated gingerroot	1 tsp.	5 mL
(or 1/4 tsp., 1 mL, ground ginger)		
Chili paste (sambal oelek), optional	1 tsp.	5 mL
Fresh (or frozen, thawed)	4	4
salmon fillets, skin removed		
(4 – 5 oz., 113 – 140 g, each)		

Preheat oven to 400°F (205°C). Combine first 7 ingredients in small bowl.

Arrange fillets on baking sheet with sides, lined with greased foil. Spread honey mixture evenly over fillets. Bake for 10 to 15 minutes until fish flakes easily when tested with fork. Serves 4.

1 serving: 274 Calories; 11.9 g Total Fat (5.1 g Mono, 2.4 g Poly, 2.9 g Sat); 75 mg Cholesterol; 17 g Carbohydrate; trace Fibre; 23 g Protein; 280 mg Sodium

Pictured on page 108.

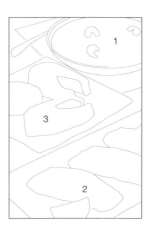

1. Seafood Tagine, page 112
2. Honey Garlic Salmon, above
3. Dill-icious Poached Salmon, page 110

Props courtesy of: Pier 1 Imports

Dill-icious Poached Salmon

Poaching is an easy, greaseless cooking method that results in moist and tender fish. The fish is gently cooked, just below the boiling point, in hot liquid.

Water	2 1/2 cups	625 mL
Dry (or alcohol-free) white wine	1/2 cup	125 mL
Prepared chicken broth	1/2 cup	125 mL
Medium lemon, sliced	1	1
Finely chopped onion	1/3 cup	75 mL
Coarsely chopped fresh dill	2 tbsp.	30 mL
(or 1 1/2 tsp., 7 mL, dried)		
Bay leaf, broken in half	1	1
Pepper	1/4 tsp.	1 mL
Salmon steaks	4	4
Butter (or hard margarine)	2 tbsp.	30 mL
All-purpose flour	2 tbsp.	30 mL
Milk	1/2 cup	125 mL
Chopped fresh dill	1 tbsp.	15 mL
(or 3/4 tsp., 4 mL, dried)		
Salt	1/4 tsp.	1 mL

Chopped fresh dill, for garnish

Combine first 8 ingredients in large frying pan. Bring to a boil. Reduce heat to low.

Place salmon in poaching liquid. Cook, covered, for about 8 minutes until fish flakes easily when tested with fork. Transfer salmon to serving plate. Cover to keep warm. Reserve 1 cup (250 mL) poaching liquid. Discard lemon slices, bay leaf and remaining poaching liquid.

Meanwhile, melt butter in medium saucepan on medium. Add flour. Heat and stir for 1 minute.

Slowly add milk, stirring constantly with whisk, until smooth. Heat and stir until boiling and thickened. Add reserved poaching liquid. Cook for 2 minutes, stirring occasionally, to blend flavours.

Add dill and salt. Stir. Pour over salmon.

Garnish with dill. Serves 4.

(continued on next page)

1 serving: 290 Calories; 17.9 g Total Fat (6.7 g Mono, 2.6 g Poly, 6.6 g Sat); 92 mg Cholesterol; 5 g Carbohydrate; trace Fibre; 24 g Protein; 320 mg Sodium

Pictured on page 108.

Artichoke Salmon

Red pepper and artichoke add a lively flavour to subtle salmon.

Can of artichoke hearts, drained	14 oz.	398 mL
Grated Parmesan cheese	3 tbsp.	50 mL
Olive (or cooking) oil	3 tbsp.	50 mL
Dried oregano	1/2 tsp.	2 mL
Pepper	1/4 tsp.	1 mL
Finely chopped roasted red pepper	1/4 cup	60 mL
Fresh (or frozen, thawed) salmon fillets, skin removed (4 – 5 oz., 113 – 140 g, each)	4	4

Preheat broiler. Put first 5 ingredients into blender or food processor. Process with on/off motion until coarsely chopped. Transfer to small bowl.

Add red pepper. Stir.

Arrange fillets on greased baking sheet with sides. Spread artichoke mixture over fillets. Broil on top rack in oven for about 8 minutes until fish flakes easily when tested with fork and top is starting to brown. Serves 4.

1 serving: 443 Calories; 29.0 g Total Fat (14.7 g Mono, 3.4 g Poly, 8.6 g Sat); 93 mg Cholesterol; 8 g Carbohydrate; 1 g Fibre; 35 g Protein; 779 mg Sodium

Seafood Tagine

Tagine is a Moroccan stew but the name also refers to the type of pot the stew is cooked in. Don't worry though, all you need to cook this sweet, fruity tagine is a saucepan. Serve on couscous or rice.

Cooking oil	1 tsp.	5 mL
Chopped onion	1 cup	250 mL
Chopped red pepper	1 cup	250 mL
Finely grated gingerroot	2 tsp.	10 mL
(or 1/2 tsp., 2 mL, ground ginger)		
Garlic cloves, minced	2	2
(or 1/2 tsp., 2 mL, powder)		
Ground cinnamon	1/2 tsp.	2 mL
Salt	1/2 tsp.	2 mL
Pepper	1/2 tsp.	2 mL
Ground cumin	1/4 tsp.	1 mL
All-purpose flour	1 tbsp.	15 mL
Prepared vegetable broth	1 cup	250 mL
Dry (or alcohol-free) white wine	1/2 cup	125 mL
Chopped dried apricot	1/4 cup	60 mL
Raisins	1/4 cup	60 mL
Liquid honey	2 tbsp.	30 mL
Lemon juice	2 tsp.	10 mL
Frozen, uncooked medium shrimp	1/2 lb.	225 g
(peeled and deveined), thawed		
Fresh (or frozen, thawed) small bay scallops	6 oz.	170 g

Heat cooking oil in medium saucepan on medium. Add next 8 ingredients. Cook for about 5 minutes, stirring occasionally, until onion starts to soften.

Add flour. Heat and stir for 1 minute.

Slowly add broth, stirring constantly, until smooth. Add next 5 ingredients. Heat and stir until boiling and thickened. Reduce heat to medium-low. Simmer, uncovered, for 5 minutes, stirring constantly, to blend flavours.

Add shrimp and scallops. Stir. Cook for about 2 minutes until shrimp turn pink and scallops are opaque. Makes about 4 cups (1 L).

1 cup (250 mL): 259 Calories; 2.8 g Total Fat (0.8 g Mono, 0.9 g Poly, 0.4 g Sat); 100 mg Cholesterol; 34 g Carbohydrate; 3 g Fibre; 21 g Protein; 571 mg Sodium

Pictured on page 108.

Rum Runner Shrimp

The rum and sweet pineapple in this shrimp dish will leave
you thinking easy, breezy tropical thoughts. (Cooking with alcohol
will flavour dishes with the essence of that particular liquor—most
of the time the actual alcohol content is evaporated.)

Butter (or hard margarine)	2 tbsp.	30 mL
Garlic cloves, minced	2	2
(or 1/2 tsp., 2 mL, powder)		
Frozen, uncooked large shrimp	1 lb.	454 g
(peeled and deveined), thawed		
Reserved pineapple juice	1/3 cup	75 mL
Dark (navy) rum	3 tbsp.	50 mL
Lime juice	3 tbsp.	50 mL
Brown sugar, packed	1 tbsp.	15 mL
Cornstarch	1 tsp.	5 mL
Grated lime zest	1/2 tsp.	2 mL
Chili paste (sambal oelek)	1/4 tsp.	1 mL
Can of pineapple chunks,	14 oz.	398 mL
drained and juice reserved		
Chopped green onion	1/4 cup	60 mL

Melt butter in large frying pan on medium. Add garlic. Heat and stir
for about 1 minute until fragrant. Add shrimp. Cook for about 3 minutes,
stirring often, until shrimp start to turn pink. Transfer to plate using slotted
spoon. Cover to keep warm.

Combine next 7 ingredients in small bowl. Add to same frying pan.
Bring to a boil on medium. Cook for about 2 minutes, stirring constantly,
until sauce starts to thicken.

Add pineapple and shrimp. Cook for about 2 minutes, stirring occasionally,
until heated through.

Sprinkle green onion over top. Makes about 4 cups (1 L).

1 cup (250 mL): 287 Calories; 7.8 g Total Fat (1.8 g Mono, 1.0 g Poly, 4.0 g Sat);
187 mg Cholesterol; 25 g Carbohydrate; 1 g Fibre; 24 g Protein; 218 mg Sodium

Garlic Clam Linguine

*We're not going to clam up about this one. How often do you get served
a clam entree at someone's home? This is a neat dinner treat.
And if you're in a real big rush, use 1/4 cup (60 mL)
of real bacon bits in place of the diced bacon and substitute
about 1 tsp. (5 mL) olive oil for the bacon drippings.*

Water	12 cups	3 L
Salt	1 1/2 tsp.	7 mL
Linguine	14 oz.	395 g
Olive oil	1 tbsp.	15 mL
Bacon slices, diced	3	3
Finely chopped onion	1/3 cup	75 mL
Garlic cloves, minced	3	3
Can of whole baby clams (with juice)	5 oz.	142 g
Dry (or alcohol-free) white wine	1/2 cup	125 mL
Pepper	1/2 tsp.	2 mL
Chopped fresh parsley	1/4 cup	60 mL
Grated Parmesan cheese	2 tbsp.	30 mL
Chopped fresh basil	1 tbsp.	15 mL

Combine water and salt in Dutch oven or large pot. Bring to a boil.
Add pasta. Boil, uncovered, for about 10 minutes, stirring occasionally,
until tender but firm. Drain, reserving 1/2 cup (125 mL) cooking water.
Return to same pot. Add olive oil. Toss until coated. Cover to keep warm.

Meanwhile, cook bacon in large frying pan on medium for about
4 minutes until crisp.

Add onion and garlic. Cook for about 2 minutes, stirring often, until onion
is softened.

Add next 3 ingredients. Stir. Bring to a boil on medium. Cook for 2 minutes
to blend flavours. Add to pasta. Toss.

Sprinkle with remaining 3 ingredients. Toss, adding reserved cooking water
a little at a time, if needed, to moisten. Makes about 6 cups (1.5 L).

*1 cup (250 mL): 402 Calories; 12.0 g Total Fat (6.3 g Mono, 1.2 g Poly, 5.7 g Sat);
34 mg Cholesterol; 53 g Carbohydrate; 2 g Fibre; 18 g Protein; 437 mg Sodium*

Fish Tacos

If you travel down Mexico way, you'll find that fish tacos are very popular.
Paired with a spicy avocado, mango and tomato salsa, they're well worth it.

Haddock fillets, any small bones removed	1 lb.	454 g
Salt, sprinkle		
Pepper, sprinkle		
Hard taco shells	8	8
Diced ripe avocado	1 cup	250 mL
Diced tomato	2/3 cup	150 mL
Mango chutney, larger pieces chopped	1/3 cup	75 mL
Lime juice	1 tbsp.	15 mL
Dried crushed chilies	1/2 tsp.	2 mL

Preheat oven to 400°F (205°C). Arrange fillets on greased baking sheet with sides. Sprinkle with salt and pepper. Bake for about 8 minutes until fish flakes easily when tested with fork. Cut into bite-sized pieces.

Meanwhile, arrange taco shells on separate ungreased baking sheet. Place in hot oven for about 5 minutes until warm.

Combine remaining 5 ingredients in medium bowl. Arrange fish in taco shells. Spoon avocado mixture over top. Makes 8 tacos.

1 taco: 160 Calories; 6.6 g Total Fat (1.9 g Mono, 0.5 g Poly, 1.2 g Sat); 32 mg Cholesterol; 14 g Carbohydrate; 2 g Fibre; 12 g Protein; 190 mg Sodium

Thoroughly Modern Chili

Forget everything you know about chili—this modern take has scallops, clams, lentils and a mild heat from chipotle peppers. Serve with rolls or Feta Polenta Muffins, page 74.

Cooking oil	2 tsp.	10 mL
Chopped onion	1 cup	250 mL
Chopped red pepper	1 cup	250 mL
Garlic cloves, minced	2	2
(or 1/2 tsp., 2 mL, powder)		
Can of lentils, rinsed and drained	19 oz.	540 mL
Tomato sauce	2 cups	500 mL
Dry (or alcohol-free) white wine	1/2 cup	125 mL
Chili powder	1 tsp.	5 mL
Finely chopped chipotle peppers	1 tsp.	5 mL
in adobo sauce (see Coach, page 133)		
Ground cumin	1/2 tsp.	2 mL
Salt	1/2 tsp.	2 mL
Fresh (or frozen, thawed) small bay scallops	1/2 lb.	225 g
Can of diced tomatoes, drained	14 oz.	398 mL
Can of whole baby clams, drained	5 oz.	142 g
Lime juice	1 tbsp.	15 mL
Chopped fresh cilantro or parsley	2 tsp.	10 mL

Heat cooking oil in large saucepan on medium-high. Add next 3 ingredients. Cook for about 5 minutes, stirring occasionally, until onion is softened.

Add next 7 ingredients. Stir. Bring to a boil. Reduce heat to medium. Boil gently, uncovered, for about 5 minutes until thickened.

Add scallops. Stir. Cook for about 3 minutes until scallops are opaque.

Add remaining 4 ingredients. Heat and stir for 1 minute. Makes about 8 cups (2 L).

1 cup (250 mL): 160 Calories; 2.2 g Total Fat (0.7 g Mono, 0.5 g Poly, 0.3 g Sat); 24 mg Cholesterol; 20 g Carbohydrate; 7 g Fibre; 13 g Protein; 857 mg Sodium

Pictured on page 89.

Cioppino

*Cioppino (pronounced chuh-PEE-noh) is a hearty tomato and seafood soup.
Our version is so hearty, you can actually serve it over pasta. Or eat it the
traditional way with some crusty rolls.*

Cooking oil	1 tbsp.	15 mL
Chopped onion	1 1/2 cups	375 mL
Sliced fresh white mushrooms	1 1/2 cups	375 mL
Chopped red pepper	1 cup	250 mL
Garlic cloves, minced	2	2
(or 1/2 tsp., 2 mL, powder)		
Dry (or alcohol-free) white wine	1/4 cup	60 mL
Can of chunky tomatoes (with juice)	19 oz.	540 mL
Tomato paste (see Coach, page 79)	2 tbsp.	30 mL
Granulated sugar	1 tsp.	5 mL
Italian seasoning	1 tsp.	5 mL
Salt	1/4 tsp.	1 mL
Fresh (or frozen, thawed) salmon fillets,	1/2 lb.	225 g
skin removed, cut into 1 inch (2.5 cm) cubes		
Fresh (or frozen, thawed) small bay scallops	1/2 lb.	225 g
Frozen, uncooked medium shrimp	1/2 lb.	225 g
(peeled and deveined), thawed		

Heat cooking oil in large frying pan on medium-high. Add next 4 ingredients.
Cook for about 5 minutes, stirring occasionally, until onion is softened.

Add wine. Stir. Add next 5 ingredients. Stir. Bring to a boil. Reduce heat to
medium. Boil gently, uncovered, for about 5 minutes until slightly thickened.

Add remaining 3 ingredients. Stir. Boil gently, uncovered, for about 5 minutes,
stirring occasionally, until fish flakes easily when tested with fork, shrimp
turn pink and scallops are opaque. Makes about 7 cups (1.75 L).

*1 cup (250 mL): 211 Calories; 6.3 g Total Fat (2.7 g Mono, 1.6 g Poly, 1.1 g Sat);
81 mg Cholesterol; 16 g Carbohydrate; 2 g Fibre; 21 g Protein; 547 mg Sodium*

COACH

Be careful not to overcook seafood. Overcooking
makes it too tough and chewy.

Honey Pecan Pasta

Taste the unexpected in this stylish pesto-dressed linguine with toasted honey pecans.

Water	8 cups	2 L
Salt	1 tsp.	5 mL
Linguine	8 oz.	225 g
Chopped pecans	1 cup	250 mL
Butter (or hard margarine)	1 tbsp.	15 mL
Honey	2 tbsp.	30 mL
Basil pesto	1/3 cup	75 mL
Chopped fresh parsley	2 tbsp.	30 mL
Lemon juice	1 tbsp.	15 mL
Salt	1/4 tsp.	1 mL
Pepper	1/4 tsp.	1 mL

Combine water and salt in large saucepan or Dutch oven. Bring to a boil. Add pasta. Boil, uncovered, for about 10 minutes, stirring occasionally, until tender but firm. Drain. Return to same pot. Cover to keep warm.

Meanwhile, heat large frying pan on medium. Add pecans. Cook for about 5 minutes, stirring occasionally, until toasted. Add butter. Heat and stir until melted. Add honey. Stir until coated. Add to pasta. Toss.

Add remaining 5 ingredients. Toss until coated. Makes about 4 cups (1 L).

1 cup (250 mL): 533 Calories; 31.0 g Total Fat (12.7 g Mono, 6.5 g Poly, 4.8 g Sat); 10 mg Cholesterol; 56 g Carbohydrate; 5 g Fibre; 12 g Protein; 306 mg Sodium

Pictured on front cover and on page 125.

Parsley can be quite a problem—recipes only call for small amounts, yet it's sold in bountiful bundles. What are you supposed to do with the leftover parsley? Wash and chop what you don't think you'll be using in the next few days, and fill an ice cube tray 3/4 full of parsley and cover with water. Then freeze to have individual parsley cubes at your disposal. When you need parsley just let the ice cube thaw and blot the leaves. This trick works great with many fresh herbs.

Sweet Potato Lentil Stew

Sweet potatoes add an unexpected flavour to this delightful stew—and unlike traditional stews, this one doesn't need to simmer for hours on end.

Cooking oil	1 tbsp.	15 mL
Chopped eggplant (with peel)	2 cups	500 mL
Chopped onion	2 cups	500 mL
Sliced celery	1 cup	250 mL
Garlic clove, minced	1	1
(or 1/4 tsp., 1 mL, powder)		
Dried oregano	1 tsp.	5 mL
Granulated sugar	1 tsp.	5 mL
Ground cumin	1 tsp.	5 mL
Salt	1/2 tsp.	2 mL
Chili powder	1/4 tsp.	1 mL
Can of lentils, rinsed and drained	19 oz.	540 mL
Can of sweet potatoes, drained and chopped	19 oz.	540 mL
Can of diced tomatoes (with juice)	14 oz.	398 mL
Prepared vegetable broth	1 cup	250 mL

Heat cooking oil in large frying pan on medium-high. Add next 4 ingredients. Cook for about 5 minutes, stirring often, until onion is softened.

Add next 5 ingredients. Heat and stir for about 1 minute until fragrant.

Add remaining 4 ingredients. Stir. Bring to a boil. Reduce heat to medium. Cook, covered, for 10 minutes, stirring occasionally, to blend flavours. Makes about 6 cups (1.5 L).

1 cup (250 mL): 254 Calories; 3.0 g Total Fat (1.4 g Mono, 0.9 g Poly, 0.3 g Sat); 0 mg Cholesterol; 50 g Carbohydrate; 14 g Fibre; 9 g Protein; 613 mg Sodium

Florentine Mushrooms

*If a dish is served florentine, expect there to be spinach and cheese—
and, in this case, a flashy presentation.*

Portobello mushrooms (about 4 inch, 10 cm, diameter), stems removed	4	4
Italian dressing	2 tbsp.	30 mL
Cooking oil	1 tsp.	5 mL
Box of frozen chopped spinach, thawed and squeezed dry	10 oz.	300 g
Large eggs, fork-beaten	2	2
Sun-dried tomato pesto	1/4 cup	60 mL
Pepper	3/4 tsp.	4 mL
Grated mozzarella cheese	1 cup	250 mL
Chopped green onion	1/4 cup	60 mL
Fine dry bread crumbs	1/4 cup	60 mL
Grated Parmesan cheese	1/4 cup	60 mL

Preheat oven to 400°F (205°C). Using small spoon, remove and discard gills from mushroom caps. Brush dressing on both sides of mushrooms. Place in greased 9 × 13 inch (22 × 33 cm) baking dish. Bake for about 8 minutes until starting to soften.

Meanwhile, heat cooking oil in large frying pan on medium. Add spinach. Cook and stir for about 3 minutes until softened.

Add next 3 ingredients. Cook and stir for about 1 minute until egg starts to set. Remove from heat.

Add next 3 ingredients. Stir until just combined. Spoon egg mixture into mushrooms.

Sprinkle Parmesan cheese over top. Bake for about 10 minutes until cheese is melted and golden. Makes 4 stuffed mushrooms.

1 stuffed mushroom: 402 Calories; 24.9 g Total Fat (9.6 g Mono, 3.1 g Poly, 11.0 g Sat); 145 mg Cholesterol; 19 g Carbohydrate; 5 g Fibre; 28 g Protein; 1105 mg Sodium

Browned Butter Fettuccine

The simplicity of this dish is what makes it so appealing. With toasted pine nuts and a sprinkling of feta, it's perfect for those nights when you want your life, and your food, simplified.

Water	8 cups	2 L
Salt	1 tsp.	5 mL
Fettuccine	8 oz.	225 g
Snow peas, trimmed and halved	1 cup	250 mL
Butter	1/4 cup	60 mL
Pine nuts	1/2 cup	125 mL
Salt	1/8 tsp.	0.5 mL
Crumbled feta cheese	3/4 cup	175 mL

Combine water and salt in large saucepan or Dutch oven. Bring to a boil. Add fettuccine. Boil, uncovered, for 8 minutes, stirring occasionally.

Add peas. Cook for 1 to 2 minutes until fettuccine is tender but firm and peas are tender-crisp. Drain. Return to same pot. Cover to keep warm.

Meanwhile, heat butter in small frying pan on medium until melted and bubbling. Add pine nuts. Heat and stir for about 4 minutes until butter is browned and pine nuts are golden. Add to fettuccine. Add salt. Toss until coated.

Sprinkle cheese over top. Makes about 4 cups (1 l).

1 cup (250 mL): 511 Calories; 28.5 g Total Fat (8.1 g Mono, 4.9 g Poly, 13.3 g Sat); 56 mg Cholesterol; 49 g Carbohydrate; 5 g Fibre; 18 g Protein; 483 mg Sodium

COACH If a recipe calls for butter, don't think you can automatically substitute margarine and get the same results. Butter browns easier and, sometimes, just performs better.

Swift Veggie Stir-Fry

Stir-fries are well-loved and cook up in a flash—it's the chopping that eats up your time. If you're rushed, use pre-cut or frozen veggies.

Prepared vegetable broth	1/2 cup	125 mL
Hoisin sauce	3 tbsp.	50 mL
Rice vinegar	2 tbsp.	30 mL
Cornstarch	1 tbsp.	15 mL
Cooking oil	1 tbsp.	15 mL
Coleslaw mix	2 cups	500 mL
Sliced carrot	1 cup	250 mL
Sliced onion	1 cup	250 mL
Garlic cloves, minced	2	2
(or 1/2 tsp., 2 mL, powder)		
Finely grated gingerroot	1 tsp.	5 mL
(or 1/4 tsp., 1 mL, ground ginger)		
Frozen Oriental mixed vegetables	6 cups	1.5 L
Chopped red pepper	1 cup	250 mL
Chopped dry-roasted peanuts (optional)	1/4 cup	60 mL

Combine first 4 ingredients in small bowl.

Heat large frying pan or wok on medium-high until very hot. Add cooking oil. Add next 5 ingredients. Stir-fry for 3 minutes.

Add mixed vegetables and red pepper. Stir-fry for about 3 minutes until vegetables are tender-crisp. Stir cornstarch mixture. Add to vegetable mixture. Heat and stir for about 1 minute until boiling and thickened.

Sprinkle with peanuts. Makes about 5 cups (1.25 L).

1 cup (250 mL): 198 Calories; 5.1 g Total Fat (1.7 g Mono, 1.1 g Poly, 0.6 g Sat); 1 mg Cholesterol; 32 g Carbohydrate; 4 g Fibre; 6 g Protein; 905 mg Sodium

Pictured on front cover and on page 125.

COACH

Can't stand the smell of garlic on your hands? After you're done all the handling, rub used, wet coffee grounds between your hands and then rinse with water.

Mediterranean Pizza

You'll never be satisfied with delivery pizza again! Instead of throwing on a few green peppers and mushrooms and calling it vegetarian pizza, we pulled out all the stops—artichokes, sun-dried tomato, olives and feta!

Ingredient	Imperial	Metric
Prebaked pizza crust (12 inch, 30 cm, diameter)	1	1
Sun-dried tomato pesto	1/4 cup	60 mL
Grated mozzarella cheese	3/4 cup	175 mL
Jar of marinated artichoke hearts, drained, blotted dry and quartered	6 oz.	170 mL
Can of sliced black olives, drained	4 1/2 oz.	125 mL
Crumbled feta cheese	3/4 cup	175 mL
Dried crushed chilies	1/2 tsp.	2 mL
Chopped fresh basil	3 tbsp.	50 mL

Preheat oven to 450°F (230°C). Place pizza crust on ungreased 12 inch (30 cm) pizza pan. Spread pesto evenly over crust. Sprinkle mozzarella cheese over top.

Sprinkle next 4 ingredients, in order given, over mozzarella cheese. Bake for 12 to 15 minutes until heated through and cheese is golden.

Sprinkle basil over top. Cuts into 8 wedges.

1 wedge: 118 Calories; 7.5 g Total Fat (2.7 g Mono, 0.3 g Poly, 3.9 g Sat); 22 mg Cholesterol; 7 g Carbohydrate; 1 g Fibre; 6 g Protein; 508 mg Sodium

Vegetable Chili Pot

*This chili is proof positive that a vegetarian one-dish meal
can be just as filling as any meat-and-potatoes fare.*

Cooking oil	1 tbsp.	15 mL
Chopped onion	2 cups	500 mL
Sliced fresh white mushrooms	2 cups	500 mL
Chopped green pepper	1 cup	250 mL
Can of black beans, rinsed and drained	19 oz.	540 mL
Tomato pasta sauce	2 cups	500 mL
Can of red kidney beans, rinsed and drained	14 oz.	398 mL
Can of stewed tomatoes, chopped	14 oz.	398 mL
Frozen kernel corn	1 cup	250 mL
Chili powder	1 tbsp.	15 mL
Ground cumin	1 tsp.	5 mL
Salt	1/4 tsp.	1 mL
Cayenne pepper	1/4 tsp.	1 mL

Heat cooking oil in large saucepan or Dutch oven on medium-high.
Add next 3 ingredients. Cook, uncovered, for about 5 minutes, stirring
often, until onion is softened.

Add remaining 9 ingredients. Stir. Bring to a boil. Reduce heat to
medium-low. Simmer, covered, for 10 minutes, stirring occasionally,
to blend flavours. Makes about 9 cups (2.25 L).

*1 cup (250 mL): 156 Calories; 2.3 g Total Fat (1.0 g Mono, 0.6 g Poly, 0.2 g Sat); 0 mg Cholesterol;
30 g Carbohydrate; 8 g Fibre; 8 g Protein; 840 mg Sodium*

Pictured on front cover and on page 125.

1. Swift Veggie Stir-Fry, page 122
2. Honey Pecan Pasta, page 118
3. Vegetable Chili Pot, above

Props courtesy of: Stokes

Spiced Orange Ham Steaks

With ham, it's all about the glaze. This sweet clove and cinnamon-scented glaze complements the smoky ham flavour perfectly.

Brown sugar, packed	1/4 cup	60 mL
Frozen concentrated orange juice	1/4 cup	60 mL
Ground cinnamon	1/8 tsp.	0.5 mL
Ground cloves	1/8 tsp.	0.5 mL
Ham steaks (4 – 5 oz., 113 – 140 g, each)	4	4

Combine first 4 ingredients in large frying pan. Heat and stir on medium for 2 to 3 minutes until sugar is dissolved and mixture starts to thicken.

Add ham. Cook for about 5 minutes, turning at halftime, until heated through and glazed. Serves 4.

1 serving: 227 Calories; 5.2 g Total Fat (2.4 g Mono, 0.6 g Poly, 1.7 g Sat); 54 mg Cholesterol; 20 g Carbohydrate; trace Fibre; 24 g Protein; 1529 mg Sodium

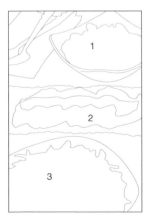

1. Hoisin Pork Stir-Fry, page 130
2. Balsamic Pork Chops, page 128
3. Orange Pork Stir-Fry, page 129

Props courtesy of: The Dazzling Gourmet
Winners Stores

Balsamic Pork Chops

Simple yet so satisfying. The sweet-and-tangy balsamic glaze enhances the natural flavours of these tender chops.

Cooking oil	2 tsp.	10 mL
Bone-in pork chops, trimmed of fat	4	4
(5 – 6 oz., 140 – 170 g, each)		
Salt	1/4 tsp.	1 mL
Pepper	1/4 tsp.	1 mL
Cooking oil	1/2 tsp.	2 mL
Finely chopped onion	1/2 cup	125 mL
Orange juice	1/2 cup	125 mL
Balsamic vinegar	3 tbsp.	50 mL
Brown sugar, packed	3 tbsp.	50 mL
Dijon mustard	1 tsp.	5 mL

Heat first amount of cooking oil in large frying pan on medium-high. Sprinkle both sides of pork with salt and pepper. Add to frying pan. Cook for about 2 minutes per side until browned. Reduce heat to medium. Cook for about 5 minutes until desired doneness. Transfer to plate. Cover to keep warm.

Add second amount of cooking oil to same frying pan. Add onion. Cook for 2 to 4 minutes, stirring often, until onion is softened and starting to brown.

Add remaining 4 ingredients. Stir. Bring to a boil. Reduce heat to medium-low. Simmer, uncovered, for 8 to 10 minutes until slightly thickened. Serve with pork. Serves 4.

1 serving: 288 Calories; 14.4 g Total Fat (6.8 g Mono, 1.8 g Poly, 4.4 g Sat); 61 mg Cholesterol; 17 g Carbohydrate; trace Fibre; 22 g Protein; 217 mg Sodium

Pictured on page 126.

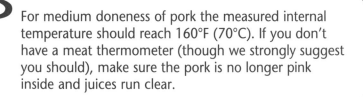

For medium doneness of pork the measured internal temperature should reach 160°F (70°C). If you don't have a meat thermometer (though we strongly suggest you should), make sure the pork is no longer pink inside and juices run clear.

Orange Pork Stir-Fry

This stir-fry is all about layering flavours. First, an initial hint of orange flavour. Second, a nice hit of chili heat. Attractive and colourful, this is an interesting and fun entree for your next dinner. Serious chili-heads can add double the amount of chili paste.

Prepared chicken broth	1/4 cup	60 mL
Cornstarch	1 tbsp.	15 mL
Orange juice	1/4 cup	60 mL
Brown sugar, packed	1 tbsp.	15 mL
Soy sauce	1 tbsp.	15 mL
Finely grated gingerroot	1 tsp.	5 mL
(or 1/4 tsp., 1 mL, ground ginger)		
Grated orange zest	1 tsp.	5 mL
Chili paste (sambal oelek)	1/2 tsp.	2 mL
Cooking oil	1 tbsp.	15 mL
Pork tenderloin, trimmed of fat, cut in half lengthwise and cut crosswise into 1/4 inch (6 mm) slices	1 lb.	454 g
Sliced red pepper	1 cup	250 mL
Thinly sliced onion	1 cup	250 mL
Fresh bean sprouts	1 cup	250 mL
Sliced green onion	1/4 cup	60 mL

Stir broth into cornstarch in small cup. Add next 6 ingredients. Stir. Set aside.

Heat large frying pan or wok on medium-high until very hot. Add cooking oil. Add pork. Stir-fry for about 5 minutes until starting to brown.

Add red pepper and onion. Stir-fry for about 3 minutes until onion is tender-crisp. Stir cornstarch mixture. Add to pork mixture. Heat and stir for about 1 minute until boiling and thickened.

Add bean sprouts and green onion. Cook and stir until heated through. Makes about 4 cups (1 L).

1 cup (250 mL): 276 Calories; 10.5 g Total Fat (4.8 g Mono, 1.8 g Poly, 2.7 g Sat); 78 mg Cholesterol; 18 g Carbohydrate; 2 g Fibre; 28 g Protein; 362 mg Sodium

Pictured on page 126.

Hoisin Pork Stir-Fry

Pork is perfect in this sweet-and-spicy peanut stir-fry.

Cooking oil	1 tbsp.	15 mL
Pork tenderloin, trimmed of fat and cut into 3/4 inch (2 cm) pieces	1 lb.	454 g
Sliced onion	1 cup	250 mL
Sliced red pepper	1 cup	250 mL
Can of sliced water chestnuts, drained	8 oz.	227 mL
Frozen peas	3/4 cup	175 mL
Hoisin sauce	1/3 cup	75 mL
Water	2 tbsp.	30 mL
Finely grated gingerroot (or 1/4 tsp., 1 mL, ground ginger)	1 tsp.	5 mL
Dried crushed chilies	1/2 tsp.	2 mL
Dry-roasted peanuts, chopped	1/4 cup	60 mL

Heat large frying pan or wok on medium-high until very hot. Add cooking oil. Add pork. Stir-fry for 2 to 3 minutes until browned.

Add next 3 ingredients. Stir-fry for 2 to 3 minutes until vegetables are tender-crisp.

Add peas. Stir.

Combine next 4 ingredients in small cup. Add to pork mixture. Heat and stir for 2 minutes.

Sprinkle peanuts over top. Makes about 5 cups (1.25 L).

1 cup (250 mL): 298 Calories; 12.7 g Total Fat (5.8 g Mono, 2.8 g Poly, 2.8 g Sat); 63 mg Cholesterol; 23 g Carbohydrate; 5 g Fibre; 24 g Protein; 345 mg Sodium

Pictured on page 126.

Stir-fries cook up mighty quickly so have all your prepared ingredients at the ready before you start cooking. Start some rice cooking before you start prepping the stir-fry, or serve the stir-fry as a filling for big lettuce leaf wraps.

Quick Pork Cassoulet

This quick and tasty version of the classic French stew
makes great cold-weather fare.

Cooking oil	1 tsp.	5 mL
Boneless fast-fry pork chops, trimmed of fat and cut into 6 pieces each	1 lb.	454 g
Seasoned salt	1/2 tsp.	2 mL
Cooking oil	1 tsp.	5 mL
Chopped carrot	1 cup	250 mL
Chopped onion	1 cup	250 mL
Chopped green pepper	1/2 cup	125 mL
Dried thyme	1 tsp.	5 mL
Garlic clove, minced (or 1/4 tsp., 1 mL, powder)	1	1
Granulated sugar	1 tsp.	5 mL
Pepper	1/4 tsp.	1 mL
Cans of mixed beans (19 oz., 540 mL, each), rinsed and drained	2	2
Can of diced tomatoes (with juice)	14 oz.	398 mL
Prepared chicken broth	1/2 cup	125 mL

Heat first amount of cooking oil in Dutch oven on medium-high. Add pork. Sprinkle with seasoned salt. Cook, uncovered, for about 3 minutes, stirring occasionally, until starting to brown. Transfer to plate. Cover to keep warm.

Add second amount of cooking oil to same pot. Add next 7 ingredients. Cook for about 3 minutes, stirring often, until onion starts to soften.

Add remaining 3 ingredients and pork. Stir, scraping any brown bits from bottom of pan. Bring to a boil. Reduce heat to medium-low. Simmer, covered, for about 10 minutes until vegetables are tender. Makes about 7 cups (1.75 L).

1 cup (250 mL): 259 Calories; 7.7 g Total Fat (3.2 g Mono, 0.9 g Poly, 2.2 g Sat); 34 mg Cholesterol; 30 g Carbohydrate; 7 g Fibre; 20 g Protein; 585 mg Sodium

Pictured on page 143 and on back cover.

Lamb Burgers

Lots of rookie cooks stay away from lamb because they think it requires special cooking techniques. It doesn't! Working with ground lamb is just like working with ground beef—but it gives burgers a whole new flavour twist. You'll find frozen ground lamb in the freezer section of your grocery store.

Fine dry bread crumbs	1/4 cup	60 mL
Steak sauce	3 tbsp.	50 mL
Chopped green onion	2 tbsp.	30 mL
Dijon mustard	1 tbsp.	15 mL
Garlic clove, minced	1	1
(or 1/4 tsp., 1 mL, powder)		
Grated lemon zest	1 tsp.	5 mL
Dried oregano	1/2 tsp.	2 mL
Salt	1/2 tsp.	2 mL
Pepper	1/4 tsp.	1 mL
Lean ground lamb	1 lb.	454 g
Mayonnaise	1/3 cup	75 mL
Chili sauce	2 tbsp.	30 mL
Hamburger buns, split	6	6

Preheat broiler. Combine first 9 ingredients in large bowl.

Add lamb. Mix well. Divide into 6 equal portions. Shape into 4 to 5 inch (10 to 12.5 cm) diameter patties. Arrange on greased broiler pan. Broil on top rack in oven for 4 to 5 minutes per side until no longer pink inside.

Combine mayonnaise and chili sauce in small cup. Spread on cut sides of bun halves. Serve patties in buns. Makes 6 burgers.

1 burger: 423 Calories; 26.3 g Total Fat (11.4 g Mono, 4.4 g Poly, 8.7 g Sat); 59 mg Cholesterol; 28 g Carbohydrate; 1 g Fibre; 17 g Protein; 707 mg Sodium

BEEF BURGERS: Use same amount of lean ground beef instead of lamb.

COACH

If you don't have a broiler pan, place a greased wire rack in a baking sheet with sides.

Turbo-Charged Macaroni

Bacon, tomato and chipotle pepper rev up this mac and cheese.
Serve with a green salad for a complete meal.

Water	12 cups	3 L
Salt	1 1/2 tsp.	7 mL
Elbow macaroni	3 cups	750 mL
Bacon slices, diced	8	8
Garlic cloves, minced	2	2
(or 1/2 tsp., 2 mL, powder)		
Can of tomato sauce	25 oz.	680 mL
Salsa	1/2 cup	125 mL
Finely chopped chipotle peppers	1 tsp.	5 mL
in adobo sauce (see Coach, below)		
Grated Mexican cheese blend	2 cups	500 mL

Combine water and salt in Dutch oven. Bring to a boil. Add macaroni.
Boil, uncovered, for 6 to 8 minutes, stirring occasionally, until tender
but firm. Drain. Return to same pot. Cover to keep warm.

Meanwhile, cook bacon in large frying pan on medium for about
4 minutes until starting to brown. Add garlic. Heat and stir for about
1 minute until fragrant.

Add next 3 ingredients. Stir. Reduce heat to medium-low. Simmer, partially
covered, for 10 minutes to blend flavours. Add macaroni. Stir.

Preheat broiler. Sprinkle cheese over macaroni mixture. Broil on centre
rack in oven (see Coach, page 95) for 3 to 4 minutes until cheese is melted
and golden. Makes about 6 1/2 cups (1.6 L).

1 cup (250 mL): 481 Calories; 24.6 g Total Fat (9.0 g Mono, 2.7 g Poly, 14.7 g Sat);
49 mg Cholesterol; 47 g Carbohydrate; 3 g Fibre; 18 g Protein; 1173 mg Sodium

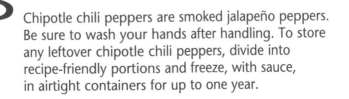

COACH

Chipotle chili peppers are smoked jalapeño peppers.
Be sure to wash your hands after handling. To store
any leftover chipotle chili peppers, divide into
recipe-friendly portions and freeze, with sauce,
in airtight containers for up to one year.

Rum Apple Pork

The perfect example of gourmet fare in minutes! These crisp pork cutlets are simply delicious with dried apples in a sweet rum sauce.

Large eggs	2	2
Fine dry bread crumbs	2/3 cup	150 mL
Paprika	1 tsp.	5 mL
Salt	1/2 tsp.	2 mL
Pepper	1/4 tsp.	1 mL
Cooking oil	1 tbsp.	15 mL
Pork cutlets (about 1 lb., 454 g)	4	4
Apple juice	2/3 cup	150 mL
Honey	1/3 cup	75 mL
Dark (navy) rum	3 tbsp.	50 mL
Brown sugar, packed	2 tbsp.	30 mL
Dijon mustard	1 tbsp.	15 mL
Soy sauce	1 tbsp.	15 mL
Dried apple	1 cup	250 mL

Beat eggs with fork in large shallow dish.

Combine next 4 ingredients in small bowl. Transfer to large plate.

Heat cooking oil in large frying pan on medium. Dip pork into egg. Press both sides of pork into bread crumb mixture until coated. Add to frying pan. Cook for about 5 minutes per side until no longer pink inside. Transfer to plate. Cover to keep warm. Remove pan from heat. Wipe clean with paper towels.

Combine next 6 ingredients in small bowl. Add to same frying pan. Bring to a boil. Reduce heat to medium-low.

Add apple. Simmer for about 5 minutes until apple is plump. Pour over pork. Serves 4.

1 serving: 558 Calories; 15.7 g Total Fat (7.3 g Mono, 2.3 g Poly, 4.4 g Sat); 146 mg Cholesterol; 75 g Carbohydrate; 4 g Fibre; 23 g Protein; 1049 mg Sodium

Ginger Mint Lamb Chops

Lamb and mint are just meant to go together. This is an easy-to-make, elegant, restaurant-style entree of thick, tender lamb chops with a fresh-tasting, sweet-and-tangy mint drizzle.

Lamb loin chops (about 2 lbs., 900 g)	8	8
Salt	1/2 tsp.	2 mL
Pepper	1/4 tsp.	1 mL
Fresh mint leaves, lightly packed	1/2 cup	125 mL
Fresh parsley leaves, lightly packed	1/2 cup	125 mL
Olive (or cooking) oil	2 tbsp.	30 mL
Lime (or orange) juice	1 tbsp.	15 mL
Liquid honey	1 tbsp.	15 mL
Ground ginger	1 tsp.	5 mL
Garlic powder	1/2 tsp.	2 mL

Preheat broiler. Sprinkle lamb with salt and pepper. Arrange on greased wire rack set in foil-lined baking sheet with sides. Broil on centre rack in oven for about 6 minutes per side until desired doneness.

Meanwhile, put remaining 7 ingredients into blender. Process until smooth. Drizzle over lamb. Serves 4.

1 serving: 517 Calories; 37.3 g Total Fat (17.7 g Mono, 2.9 g Poly, 13.9 g Sat); 131 mg Cholesterol; 10 g Carbohydrate; 2 g Fibre; 34 g Protein; 407 mg Sodium

Lamb cooked at a medium doneness will reach an internal temperature of 150°F (65°C).

Angel Delight Trifle

The first great thing about trifle is that you've obviously handcrafted it with care. The second great thing about trifle is that you don't actually have to bake a thing. The third? The strawberry-soaked fluffy cake enveloped in creamy vanilla pudding.

Torn angel food cake (bite-sized pieces)	5 cups	1.25 L
Container of frozen strawberries in light syrup, thawed	15 oz.	425 g
Box of instant vanilla pudding powder (4-serving size)	1	1
Milk	1 1/2 cups	375 mL
Frozen whipped topping, thawed	2 cups	500 mL

Put cake into large glass bowl. Spoon strawberries with syrup over cake.

Beat pudding powder and milk in medium bowl for about 2 minutes until thickened. Spread evenly over strawberries.

Spread whipped topping evenly over top. Chill for 10 minutes. Serves 8.

1 serving: 514 Calories; 5.0 g Total Fat (0.3 g Mono, 0.2 g Poly, 4.4 g Sat); 3 mg Cholesterol; 110 g Carbohydrate; trace Fibre; 11 g Protein; 950 mg Sodium

Berry Cake Cups

Sponge cake topped with citrus cream and fresh berries is sure to draw plenty of oohs and aahs from the crowd. If berries are out of season, you can use thawed, frozen mixed berries.

Block of cream cheese, softened	8 oz.	250 g
Icing (confectioner's) sugar	1/2 cup	125 mL
Lemon juice	2 tbsp.	30 mL
Grated lemon zest	2 1/2 tsp.	12 mL
Sponge cake berry cups	6	6
Fresh blueberries	1 1/2 cups	375 mL
Quartered fresh strawberries	1 1/2 cups	375 mL

(continued on next page)

136

Beat first 4 ingredients in medium bowl for about 3 minutes until smooth.

Place cake cups on 6 dessert plates. Spoon cream cheese mixture into cups.

Spoon blueberries and strawberries over cream cheese mixture. Makes 6 cake cups.

1 cake cup: 292 Calories; 15.7 g Total Fat (3.8 g Mono, 0.6 g Poly, 8.8 g Sat); 61 mg Cholesterol; 34 g Carbohydrate; 2 g Fibre; 5 g Protein; 263 mg Sodium

Pictured on page 89.

Variation: Combine blueberries and strawberries in small bowl before preparing cream cheese mixture. Add 2 tbsp. (30 mL) orange liqueur. Stir. Let stand until ready to spoon over cakes.

Chocolate Nachos

Here's your chance to get creative and turn convention on its head. Serve these crisp tortillas with cinnamon sugar and a chocolate drizzle at your next get-together and your guests will think you are oh so clever.

Granulated sugar	1/4 cup	60 mL
Ground cinnamon	2 tsp.	10 mL
Ground ginger	1/4 tsp.	1 mL
Flour tortillas (9 inch, 22 cm, diameter)	4	4
Cooking oil	2 tbsp.	30 mL
Semi-sweet chocolate chips	1/3 cup	75 mL
Sour cream	1/4 cup	60 mL

Preheat oven to 350°F (175°C). Combine first 3 ingredients in small bowl.

Brush tortillas with cooking oil. Sprinkle cinnamon mixture over top. Cut tortillas into 8 wedges each. Arrange wedges in single layer on 2 greased baking sheets with sides. Bake on separate racks in oven for about 10 minutes, switching position of baking sheets at halftime, until edges are golden.

Meanwhile, put chocolate chips into 1 cup (250 mL) liquid measure. Microwave, uncovered, on medium (50%) for 20 to 30 seconds at a time, stirring in between, until chocolate is almost melted. Do not overheat. Add sour cream. Stir until smooth. Spoon into small resealable freezer bag with tiny piece snipped off 1 corner. Drizzle chocolate in decorative pattern over wedges. Makes 32 wedges.

1 wedge: 45 Calories; 2.4 g Total Fat (0.8 g Mono, 0.3 g Poly, 0.8 g Sat); 1 mg Cholesterol; 6 g Carbohydrate; trace Fibre; 1 g Protein; 40 mg Sodium

Chocolate Fudge Sauce

Canned just can't compare. Use hot or cold.
Store in the fridge for up to two weeks.

Butter (or hard margarine)	1/2 cup	125 mL
Granulated sugar	1 cup	250 mL
Cocoa, sifted if lumpy	3/4 cup	175 mL
Evaporated milk (or half-and-half cream)	2/3 cup	150 mL
Vanilla extract	2 tsp.	10 mL

Melt butter in medium saucepan on medium.

Whisk sugar and cocoa into butter. Slowly add evaporated milk, stirring constantly with whisk, until smooth. Heat and stir for about 4 minutes until boiling. Remove from heat.

Add vanilla. Stir. Makes about 2 cups (500 mL).

1/2 cup (125 mL): 467 Calories; 25.6 g Total Fat (6.8 g Mono, 1.0 g Poly, 16.1 g Sat); 63 mg Cholesterol; 61 g Carbohydrate; 4 g Fibre; 6 g Protein; 212 mg Sodium

Waffles Pseudo-Suzette

No time to make crepes? Substitute frozen waffles and you have a sweet dessert (or extra-special brunch treat) with a delicious creamsicle taste.

ORANGE SAUCE

Butter (or hard margarine)	1/2 cup	125 mL
Granulated sugar	1/4 cup	60 mL
Orange juice	1 cup	250 mL
Grated orange zest	2 tsp.	10 mL
Orange liqueur (optional)	1/4 cup	60 mL
Blueberry (or plain) frozen waffles	4	4
Vanilla frozen yogurt	2 cups	500 mL

Orange Sauce: Heat butter and sugar in small saucepan on medium-high, stirring occasionally, until butter is melted. Add next 3 ingredients. Stir. Bring to a boil. Reduce heat to medium. Cook for about 7 minutes, stirring occasionally, until mixture is slightly thickened. Makes about 1 cup (250 mL) sauce.

(continued on next page)

Meanwhile, toast waffles. Place waffles on 4 dessert plates. Spoon frozen yogurt over waffles. Spoon Orange Sauce over top. Serves 4.

1 serving: 485 Calories; 29.9 g Total Fat (7.1 g Mono, 1.0 g Poly, 17.6 g Sat); 69 mg Cholesterol; 51 g Carbohydrate; 1 g Fibre; 6 g Protein; 410 mg Sodium

Pecan Raisin Tarts

This traditional nut and raisin tart is the perfect dessert to put out at holiday gatherings. Guaranteed to disappear quickly!

Large egg	1	1
Brown sugar, packed	1/2 cup	125 mL
Coarsely chopped raisins	1/4 cup	60 mL
Corn syrup	1/4 cup	60 mL
Butter (or hard margarine), softened	3 tbsp.	50 mL
Finely chopped pecans	2 tbsp.	30 mL
Lemon juice	1 1/2 tsp.	7 mL
Vanilla extract	1/2 tsp.	2 mL
Salt	1/8 tsp.	0.5 mL
Unbaked tart shells	12	12

Preheat oven to 375°F (190°C). Beat egg with fork in medium bowl until frothy. Add next 8 ingredients. Stir well.

Arrange tart shells on baking sheet with sides. Spoon raisin mixture into tart shells. Bake on bottom rack in oven for about 15 minutes until pastry is browned and filling rises to form a dome. Remove tarts from baking sheet and place on wire rack to cool. Makes 12 tarts.

1 tart: 202 Calories; 10.4 g Total Fat (4.4 g Mono, 1.2 g Poly, 4.0 g Sat); 23 mg Cholesterol; 27 g Carbohydrate; 1 g Fibre; 2 g Protein; 187 mg Sodium

Pictured on page 17.

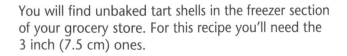

COACH

You will find unbaked tart shells in the freezer section of your grocery store. For this recipe you'll need the 3 inch (7.5 cm) ones.

Vanilla Rice Pudding

This nostalgic fave with sweet, plump raisins and a hint of vanilla is sure to coax a sigh of contentment from your family and friends.

Water	1 cup	250 mL
Raisins	1/4 cup	60 mL
Instant rice	1 cup	250 mL
Salt	1/4 tsp.	1 mL
Box of instant vanilla pudding powder (4-serving size)	1	1
Ground nutmeg	1/8 tsp.	0.5 mL
Milk	2 cups	500 mL

Place medium plastic bowl in freezer. Combine water and raisins in medium saucepan. Bring to a boil. Add rice and salt. Stir. Remove from heat. Let stand, covered, for 5 minutes. Transfer to chilled bowl. Chill in freezer for 5 minutes.

Combine pudding powder and nutmeg in large bowl. Add milk. Beat for about 2 minutes until thickened. Add cooled rice mixture in 2 additions, stirring well after each addition. Chill in freezer for 10 minutes. Makes about 4 cups (1 L).

1 cup (250 mL): 265 Calories; 1.5 g Total Fat (0.6 g Mono, 0.1 g Poly, 0.8 g Sat); 8 mg Cholesterol; 57 g Carbohydrate; 1 g Fibre; 7 g Protein; 582 mg Sodium

Quick Fruit Crumble

Using canned fruit and filling makes quick work of this sweet crumble.

Coarsely crushed vanilla wafers (about 25 wafers)	1 cup	250 mL
Plain spreadable cream cheese	1/3 cup	75 mL
Chopped pecans	1/4 cup	60 mL
Can of apple pie filling	19 oz.	540 mL
Can of sliced peaches in syrup, drained	14 oz.	398 mL
Ground ginger	1/2 tsp.	2 mL
Ground cinnamon	1/4 tsp.	1 mL

Preheat oven to 400°F (205°C). Measure first 3 ingredients into medium bowl. Stir until mixture resembles coarse crumbs.

(continued on next page)

140 Sweets & Treats

Combine remaining 4 ingredients in large bowl. Spoon into greased 2 quart (2 L) shallow baking dish. Sprinkle crumb mixture over top. Bake for about 15 minutes until bubbling and golden. Serves 4.

1 serving: 434 Calories; 16.0 g Total Fat (6.0 g Mono, 1.9 g Poly, 5.5 g Sat); 25 mg Cholesterol; 74 g Carbohydrate; 5 g Fibre; 4 g Protein; 196 mg Sodium

Pictured on page 143.

Don't confuse vanilla wafers with the popular ice cream wafers found with other sugary cookies. Vanilla wafers, although also found in the cookie aisle, come in a cardboard box and look like plain round cookies.

Strawberries And Cream Sauce

Guests will be delighted with this simply elegant fresh dessert.

Cream cheese, softened	4 oz.	125 g
Granulated sugar	2/3 cup	150 mL
Milk	1/2 cup	125 mL
Vanilla extract	1 1/2 tbsp.	25 mL
Sliced fresh strawberries	3 cups	750 mL

Beat cream cheese and sugar in small bowl until smooth.

Slowly add milk and vanilla, beating constantly, until sugar is dissolved.

Put strawberries into a medium bowl. Spoon cream cheese mixture over top. Makes about 4 cups (1 L).

1 cup (250 mL): 291 Calories; 10.6 g Total Fat (3.0 g Mono, 0.6 g Poly, 6.4 g Sat); 33 mg Cholesterol; 45 g Carbohydrate; 2 g Fibre; 4 g Protein; 102 mg Sodium

Always rinse your strawberries before hulling to avoid getting them waterlogged.

Caramel Pineapple Sundaes

Pining for pineapple? The flavours of caramel and tropical fruit combine in this easy dessert option. Store extra sauce in an airtight container in the fridge for up to two weeks. Microwave for 20 to 30 seconds to warm.

CARAMEL PINEAPPLE SAUCE

Brown sugar, packed	1/2 cup	125 mL
Butter (or hard margarine)	3 tbsp.	50 mL
Half-and-half cream	1/3 cup	75 mL
Can of pineapple tidbits, drained	14 oz.	398 mL
Vanilla ice cream	2 cups	500 mL

Caramel Pineapple Sauce: Heat brown sugar and butter in small saucepan on medium for 4 to 5 minutes, stirring occasionally, until brown sugar is dissolved.

Add cream. Stir. Bring to a boil on medium. Boil gently for about 5 minutes, stirring occasionally, until mixture is thickened.

Add pineapple. Stir. Makes about 1 2/3 cups (400 mL) sauce.

Spoon ice cream into 4 dessert bowls. Spoon Caramel Pineapple Sauce over top. Makes 4 sundaes.

1 sundae: 525 Calories; 28.9 g Total Fat (2.9 g Mono, 0.4 g Poly, 17.9 g Sat); 150 mg Cholesterol; 61 g Carbohydrate; 1 g Fibre; 6 g Protein; 158 mg Sodium

PINEAPPLE BANANA SPLITS: Cut 4 bananas in half lengthwise. Place 1 half on each side of ice cream in dessert bowls. Add 1/4 cup (60 mL) sliced strawberries to each bowl. Pour sauce over top.

1. Quick Fruit Crumble, page 140
2. Lentil Feta Salad, page 50
3. Quick Pork Cassoulet, page 131

Props courtesy of: Casa Bugatti

Double Chocolate Minis

Get your chocolate fix, and double it for good measure, with these moist, chocolatey brownies bursting with chocolate chips.

All-purpose flour	3/4 cup	175 mL
Cocoa, sifted if lumpy	1/2 cup	125 mL
Salt	1/4 tsp.	1 mL
Large eggs	2	2
Granulated sugar	1 cup	250 mL
Butter (or hard margarine), melted	1/3 cup	75 mL
Semi-sweet chocolate chips	1 cup	250 mL

Preheat oven to 350°F (175°C). Combine first 3 ingredients in small bowl.

Whisk next 3 ingredients in medium bowl until combined. Add flour mixture. Stir well.

Add chocolate chips. Stir. Fill 24 greased and floured mini-muffin cups 3/4 full. Bake for about 15 minutes until wooden pick inserted in centre of brownie comes out moist but not wet with batter. Do not overbake. Makes 24 mini-brownies.

1 mini-brownie: 129 Calories; 5.8 g Total Fat (0.9 g Mono, 0.2 g Poly, 3.5 g Sat); 22 mg Cholesterol; 18 g Carbohydrate; 1 g Fibre; 2 g Protein; 48 mg Sodium

Pictured on page 144.

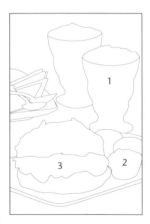

1. Tiramisu Parfaits, page 147
2. Double Chocolate Minis, above
3. Peach Strawberry Shortcakes, page 146

Props courtesy of: Winners Stores

Peach Strawberry Shortcakes

This traditional biscuit shortcake is tall on flavour and delightfully presented.

Biscuit mix	2 1/4 cups	550 mL
Buttermilk (or soured milk, see Coach, page 42)	1/2 cup	125 mL
Butter (or hard margarine), melted	1/4 cup	60 mL
Granulated sugar	1/4 cup	60 mL
Sliced fresh strawberries	3 cups	750 mL
Can of sliced peaches in light syrup, drained and chopped	14 oz.	398 mL
Icing (confectioner's) sugar (optional)	2 tbsp.	30 mL
Frozen whipped topping, thawed	3 cups	750 mL
Slivered almonds, toasted (see Coach, page 63), optional	1/4 cup	60 mL

Preheat oven to 400°F (205°C). Measure first 4 ingredients into large bowl. Stir until soft dough forms. Spoon into 6 mounds on greased baking sheet with sides. Bake for about 10 minutes until golden. Remove baking sheet to wire rack. Cool slightly.

Meanwhile, combine next 3 ingredients in small bowl.

Cut biscuits in half horizontally. Place bottom halves on 6 dessert plates. Top with 1/4 cup (60 mL) whipped topping. Spoon fruit mixture over top. Place top halves of biscuits over fruit mixture. Spoon remaining whipped topping over top.

Sprinkle with almonds. Makes 6 shortcakes.

1 shortcake: 688 Calories; 34.6 g Total Fat (10.6 g Mono, 2.5 g Poly, 17.5 g Sat); 22 mg Cholesterol; 88 g Carbohydrate; 5 g Fibre; 11 g Protein; 1055 mg Sodium

Pictured on page 144.

Tiramisu Parfaits

*This is tiramisu without the fuss. The Tuscan truffle, as it is sometimes called,
is an irresistible confection of creamy, smooth chocolate and coffee flavours.*

Cold strong prepared coffee	3/4 cup	175 mL
Rum extract	1 tsp.	5 mL
Vanilla extract	1 tsp.	5 mL
Tub of light cream cheese	8 oz.	250 g
Vanilla yogurt	1 cup	250 mL
Coarsely crushed vanilla wafers (about 40 wafers)	1 1/2 cups	375 mL
Cocoa, sifted if lumpy	2 tsp.	10 mL

Combine first 3 ingredients in small cup. Set aside.

Beat cream cheese in small bowl until smooth. Add yogurt. Mix well.

To assemble, layer ingredients in 4 dessert bowls as follows:

1. 3 tbsp. (50 mL) wafer crumbs

2. 2 tbsp. (30 mL) coffee mixture

3. 1/4 cup (60 mL) cream cheese mixture

4. 2 tbsp. (30 mL) wafer crumbs

5. 1 tbsp. (15 mL) coffee mixture

6. 3 tbsp. (50 mL) cream cheese mixture

Sprinkle 1/2 tsp. (2 mL) cocoa over each parfait. Makes 4 parfaits.

*1 parfait: 526 Calories; 32.3 g Total Fat (12.3 g Mono, 2.2 g Poly, 16.0 g Sat); 66 mg Cholesterol;
49 g Carbohydrate; 1 g Fibre; 10 g Protein; 392 mg Sodium*

Pictured on page 144.

Maple Apple Muffins

These pretty muffins are full of apple, maple and cinnamon. Best served warm.

All-purpose flour	2 1/4 cups	550 mL
Baking powder	1 tbsp.	15 mL
Ground cinnamon	1 1/2 tsp.	7 mL
Salt	1 tsp.	5 mL
Large eggs	3	3
Brown sugar, packed	1 cup	250 mL
Applesauce	3/4 cup	175 mL
Cooking oil	1/3 cup	75 mL
Maple (or maple-flavoured) syrup	1/3 cup	75 mL
Maple (or maple-flavoured) syrup	2 tbsp.	30 mL

Preheat oven to 375°F (190°C). Measure first 4 ingredients into medium bowl. Stir. Make a well in centre.

Whisk next 5 ingredients in small bowl until combined. Add to well. Stir until just moistened. Fill 12 greased muffin cups 3/4 full. Bake for 18 to 20 minutes until wooden pick inserted in centre of muffin comes out clean.

Brush with second amount of syrup. Let stand in pan for 5 minutes. Remove muffins from pan and place on wire rack to cool. Makes 12 muffins.

1 muffin: 261 Calories; 7.4 g Total Fat (4.1 g Mono, 2.0 g Poly, 0.8 g Sat); 47 mg Cholesterol; 46 g Carbohydrate; 1 g Fibre; 4 g Protein; 284 mg Sodium

Very Berry Melon Cooler

A refreshing drink—and a perfect way to use up any leftover watermelon.

Chopped watermelon	2 cups	500 mL
Frozen whole strawberries	2 cups	500 mL
Ginger ale	1/3 cup	75 mL
Lemon juice	3 tbsp.	50 mL
Granulated sugar	2 tbsp.	30 mL
Ice cubes	6	6

(continued on next page)

Put first 5 ingredients into blender. Process until smooth.

Add ice cubes, one at a time, processing after each addition until smooth. Makes about 3 1/2 cups (875 mL).

1 cup (250 mL): 174 Calories; 0.2 g Total Fat (trace Mono, 0.1 g Poly, trace Sat); 0 mg Cholesterol; 48 g Carbohydrate; 3 g Fibre; 1 g Protein; 6 mg Sodium

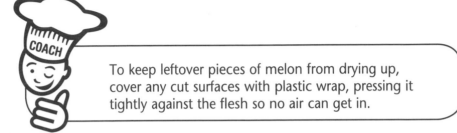

To keep leftover pieces of melon from drying up, cover any cut surfaces with plastic wrap, pressing it tightly against the flesh so no air can get in.

Dried Fruit Dips

The newest chocolate-dipped darlings are all dried up. This treat is very unique.

Milk chocolate melting wafers	3/4 cup	175 mL
Dried apricots, mango, papaya and pineapple, cut into 2-bite pieces	8 oz.	225 g

Place chocolate wafers in small microwave-safe bowl. Microwave, uncovered, on medium (50%) for 1 minute. Stir. Microwave, uncovered, on medium (50%) for 20 to 30 seconds at a time, stirring in between, until chocolate is almost melted. Do not overheat. Stir until smooth.

Dip fruit pieces about halfway into chocolate. Place on waxed paper for about 10 minutes until set. Makes about 32 pieces.

1 piece: 48 Calories; 1.5 g Total Fat (0 g Mono, 0 g Poly, 1.0 g Sat); 0 mg Cholesterol; 9 g Carbohydrate; 1 g Fibre; 1 g Protein; 4 mg Sodium

Variation: Use white or dark chocolate melting wafers instead.

If your chocolate has become too thick for dipping, microwave for five seconds on medium. Stir.

Measurement Tables

Throughout this book measurements are given in Conventional and Metric measure. To compensate for differences between the two measurements due to rounding, a full metric measure is not always used. The cup used is the standard 8 fluid ounce. Temperature is given in degrees Fahrenheit and Celsius. Baking pan measurements are in inches and centimetres as well as quarts and litres. An exact metric conversion is given below as well as the working equivalent (Metric Standard Measure).

Spoons

Conventional Measure	Metric Exact Conversion Millilitre (mL)	Metric Standard Measure Millilitre (mL)
1/8 teaspoon (tsp.)	0.6 mL	0.5 mL
1/4 teaspoon (tsp.)	1.2 mL	1 mL
1/2 teaspoon (tsp.)	2.4 mL	2 mL
1 teaspoon (tsp.)	4.7 mL	5 mL
2 teaspoons (tsp.)	9.4 mL	10 mL
1 tablespoon (tbsp.)	14.2 mL	15 mL

Cups

Conventional Measure	Metric Exact Conversion Millilitre (mL)	Metric Standard Measure Millilitre (mL)
1/4 cup (4 tbsp.)	56.8 mL	60 mL
1/3 cup (5 1/3 tbsp.)	75.6 mL	75 mL
1/2 cup (8 tbsp.)	113.7 mL	125 mL
2/3 cup (10 2/3 tbsp.)	151.2 mL	150 mL
3/4 cup (12 tbsp.)	170.5 mL	175 mL
1 cup (16 tbsp.)	227.3 mL	250 mL
4 1/2 cups	1022.9 mL	1000 mL (1 L)

Dry Measurements

Conventional Measure Ounces (oz.)	Metric Exact Conversion Grams (g)	Metric Standard Measure Grams (g)
1 oz.	28.3 g	28 g
2 oz.	56.7 g	57 g
3 oz.	85.0 g	85 g
4 oz.	113.4 g	125 g
5 oz.	141.7 g	140 g
6 oz.	170.1 g	170 g
7 oz.	198.4 g	200 g
8 oz.	226.8 g	250 g
16 oz.	453.6 g	500 g
32 oz.	907.2 g	1000 g (1 kg)

Oven Temperatures

Fahrenheit (°F)	Celsius (°C)
175°	80°
200°	95°
225°	110°
250°	120°
275°	140°
300°	150°
325°	160°
350°	175°
375°	190°
400°	205°
425°	220°
450°	230°
475°	240°
500°	260°

Pans

Conventional Inches	Metric Centimetres
8x8 inch	20x20 cm
9x9 inch	22x22 cm
9x13 inch	22x33 cm
10x15 inch	25x38 cm
11x17 inch	28x43 cm
8x2 inch round	20x5 cm
9x2 inch round	22x5 cm
10x4 1/2 inch tube	25x11 cm
8x4x3 inch loaf	20x10x7.5 cm
9x5x3 inch loaf	22x12.5x7.5 cm

Casseroles

CANADA & BRITAIN Standard Size Casserole	Exact Metric Measure	UNITED STATES Standard Size Casserole	Exact Metric Measure
1 qt. (5 cups)	1.13 L	1 qt. (4 cups)	900 mL
1 1/2 qts. (7 1/2 cups)	1.69 L	1 1/2 qts. (6 cups)	1.35 L
2 qts. (10 cups)	2.25 L	2 qts. (8 cups)	1.8 L
2 1/2 qts. (12 1/2 cups)	2.81 L	2 1/2 qts. (10 cups)	2.25 L
3 qts. (15 cups)	3.38 L	3 qts. (12 cups)	2.7 L
4 qts. (20 cups)	4.5 L	4 qts. (16 cups)	3.6 L
5 qts. (25 cups)	5.63 L	5 qts. (20 cups)	4.5 L

Coach Index

151

Recipe Index

152

153

154

155